The Story of the Volsungs
(Volsunga Saga)

Anonymous Old Norse
and Icelandic Mythologies

Contents

INTRODUCTION 7
TRANSLATORS' PREFACE...24
THE STORY OF THE VOLSUNGS AND NIBLUNGS. 28
CHAPTER I.   Of Sigi, the Son of Odin. 28
CHAPTER II. Of the Birth of Volsung, the Son 30
CHAPTER III. Of the Sword that Sigmund 33
CHAPTER IV. How King Siggeir wedded Signy 35
CHAPTER V. Of the Slaying of King Volsung. 37
CHAPTER VI. Of how Signy sent the Children of her. 40
CHAPTER VII. Of the Birth of Sinfjotli the Son of Sigmund. ...42
CHAPTER VIII. The Death of King Siggeir and of Stigny. 44
CHAPTER IX. How Helgi, the son of Sigmund 50
CHAPTER X. The ending of Sinfjatli, Sigmund's Son. 54
CHAPTER XI. 56
CHAPTER XII. Of the Shards of the Sword Gram 59
CHAPTER XIII. Of the Birth and Waxing of Sigurd Fafnir's-bane....62
CHAPTER XIV. Regin's tale of his Brothers............................65
CHAPTER XV. 68
CHAPTER XVI. The prophecy of Grifir....................................70
CHAPTER XVII. Of Sigurd's Avenging of Sigmund his Father.....71
CHAPTER XVIII. Of the Slaying of the Worm Fafnir. 76
CHAPTER XIX. Of the Slaying of Regin, Son of Hreidmar. 80
CHAPTER XX. Of Sigurd's Meeting with Brynhild on the Mountain..............84
CHAPTER XXI. More Wise Words of Brynhild.........................91
CHAPTER XXII. Of the Semblance and Array of Sigurd Fafnir's bane. 93
CHAPTER XXIII. Sigurd comes to Hlymdale. 95
CHAPTER XXIV. Sigurd sees Brynhild at Hlymdale. 96
CHAPTER XXV. Of the Dream of Gudrun, Giuki's daughter. 99
CHAPTER XXVI. 102
CHAPTER XXVII. The Wooing of Brynhild. 105
CHAPTER XXVIII. How the Queens held angry converse together 109
CHAPTER XXIX. Of Brynhild's great Grief and Mourning. 113
CHAPTER XXX. Of the Slaying of Sigurd Fafnir's-bane...........118
CHAPTER XXXI. Of the Lamentation of Gudrun over Sigurd's dead 122
CHAPTER XXXII. Of the Ending of Brynhild...........................130
CHAPTER XXXIII. Gudrun wedded to Alii...............................133
CHAPTER XXXIV. Atli bids the Giukings to him......................137

CHAPTER XXXV. The Dreams of the Wives of the Giukings. 140
CHAPTER XXXVI. Of the Journey of the Giukings to King Atli...................... 142
CHAPTER XXXVII. The Battle in the Burg of King Atli. 145
CHAPTER XXXVIII. Of the slaying of the Giukings. 147
CHAPTER XXXIX. The End of Atli and his Kin and Folk. 150
CHAPTER XL. How Gudrun cast herself into the Sea 154
CHAPTER XLI. Of the Wedding and Slaying of Swanhild. 155
CHAPTER XLII. Gudrun sends her Sons to avenge Swanhild......................... 157
CHAPTER XLIII. The Latter End of all the Kin of the Giukings. 159
APPENDIX: EXCERPTS FROM THE POETIC EDDA. 161
PART OF THE SECOND LAY OF.. 161
HELGI HUNDINGS-BANE.. 161
PART OF THE LAY OF SIGRDRIFA.. 170
THE HELL-RIDE OF BRYNHILD.. 194
THE SONG OF ATLI. 216
THE WHETTING OF GUDRUN. 229
THE LAMENT OF ODDRUN. 245

THE STORY OF THE VOLSUNGS

BY

Anonymous Old Norse and
Icelandic Mythologies

INTRODUCTION

I t would seem fitting for a Northern folk, deriving the greater and better part of their speech, laws, and customs from a Northern root, that the North should be to them, if not a holy land, yet at least a place more to be regarded than any part of the world beside; that howsoever their knowledge widened of other men, the faith and deeds of their forefathers would never lack interest for them, but would always be kept in remembrance. One cause after another has, however, aided in turning attention to classic men and lands at the cost of our own history. Among battles, "every schoolboy" knows the story of Marathon or Salamis, while it would be hard indeed to find one who did more than recognise the name, if even that, of the great fights of Hafrsfirth or Sticklestead. The language and history of Greece and Rome, their laws and religions, have been always held part of the learning needful to an educated man, but no trouble has been taken to make him familiar with his own people or their tongue. Even that Englishman who knew Alfred, Bede, Caedmon, as well as he knew Plato, Caesar, Cicero, or Pericles, would be hard bestead were he asked about the great peoples from whom we sprang; the warring of Harold Fairhair or Saint Olaf; the Viking (1) kingdoms in these (the British) Western Isles; the settlement of Iceland, or even of Normandy. The knowledge of all these things would now be even smaller than it is among us were it not that there was one land left where the olden learning found refuge and was kept in being. In England, Germany, and the rest of Europe, what is left of the traditions of pagan times has been altered in a thousand ways by foreign influence, even as the peoples and their speech have been by the influx of foreign blood; but Iceland held to the old tongue that was once the universal speech of northern folk, and held also the great stores of tale and poem that are slowly becoming once more the common heritage of their descendants. The truth, care, and literary beauty of its records;

the varied and strong life shown alike in tale and history; and the preservation of the old speech, character, and tradition -- a people placed apart as the Icelanders have been -- combine to make valuable what Iceland holds for us. Not before 1770, when Bishop Percy translated Mallet's "Northern Antiquities", was anything known here of Icelandic, or its literature. Only within the latter part of this century has it been studied, and in the brief book-list at the end of this volume may be seen the little that has been done as yet. It is, however, becoming ever clearer, and to an increasing number, how supremely important is Icelandic as a word-hoard to the English- speaking peoples, and that in its legend, song, and story there is a very mine of noble and pleasant beauty and high manhood. That which has been done, one may hope, is but the beginning of a great new birth, that shall give back to our language and literature all that heedlessness and ignorance bid fair for awhile to destroy.

The Scando-Gothic peoples who poured southward and westward over Europe, to shake empires and found kingdoms, to meet Greek and Roman in conflict, and levy tribute everywhere, had kept up their constantly-recruited waves of incursion, until they had raised a barrier of their own blood. It was their own kin, the sons of earlier invaders, who stayed the landward march of the Northmen in the time of Charlemagne. To the Southlands their road by land was henceforth closed. Then begins the day of the Vikings, who, for two hundred years and more, "held the world at ransom." Under many and brave leaders they first of all came round the "Western Isles" (2) toward the end of the eighth century; soon after they invaded Normandy, and harried the coasts of France; gradually they lengthened their voyages until there was no shore of the then known world upon which they were unseen or unfelt. A glance at English history will show the large part of it they fill, and how they took tribute from the Anglo-Saxons, who, by the way, were far nearer kin to them than is usually thought. In Ireland, where the old civilisation was falling to pieces, they founded kingdoms at Limerick and Dublin among other places; (3) the last named, of which the first king, Olaf the White, was traditionally descended of Sigurd the Volsung, (4) endured even to the English invasion, when it was taken by men of the same Viking blood a little altered. What effect they produced upon the natives may be seen from the description given by the unknown historian of the "Wars of the Gaedhil with the Gaill": "In a word, although there were an hundred hard-steeled iron heads on one neck, and an hundred sharp, ready, cool, never-rusting brazen tongues in each head, and an hundred garrulous, loud, unceasing voices from each tongue, they could not recount, or narrate, or enumerate, or tell what all the Gaedhil suffered in common -- both men and women, laity and clergy, old and young, noble and ignoble -- of hardship, and of injury, and of oppression, in every house, from these valiant, wrathful, purely pagan people. Even though great were this cruelty, oppression, and tyranny, though numerous were the oft-victorious clans of the many- familied Erinn; though numerous their kings, and their royal chiefs, and their princes; though numerous their heroes and champions, and their brave soldiers, their chiefs of valour and renown and deeds of arms; yet not one of them was able to give relief, alleviation, or deliverance from that oppression and tyranny, from the numbers and multitudes, and the cruelty and the wrath of the brutal, ferocious, furious, untamed, implacable hordes by whom that oppression was inflicted, because of the excellence of their polished, ample, treble, heavy, trusty, glittering corslets; and their hard, strong, valiant swords; and their well-riveted long spears, and their ready, brilliant arms of valour besides; and because of the greatness of their achievements and of their deeds, their bravery, and their valour, their strength, and their venom, and their ferocity, and because of the excess of their thirst and their hunger for the brave, fruitful, nobly-inhabited, full of cataracts, rivers, bays, pure, smooth-plained, sweet grassy land of Erinn" -- (pp. 52-53). Some part of this, however, must be abated, because the chronicler is exalting the terror-striking enemy that he may still further exalt his own people, the Dal Cais, who did so much under Brian Boroimhe to check the inroads of the Northmen. When a book does (5) appear, which has been announced these ten years past, we shall have more material for the reconstruction of the life of those times than is now anywhere accessible. Viking earldoms also were the Orkneys, Faroes, and Shetlands. So late as 1171, in the reign of Henry II., the year after Beckett's murder, Earl Sweyn Asleifsson of Orkney, who had long been the terror of the western seas, "fared a sea-roving" and scoured the western coast of England, Man, and the east of Ireland, but was killed in an attack on his kinsmen of Dublin. He had used to go upon a regular plan that may be taken as typical of the homely manner of most of his like in their cruising: "Sweyn had in the spring hard work, and made them lay down very much seed, and looked much after it himself. But when that toil was ended, he fared away every spring on a viking-voyage, and harried about among the southern isles and Ireland, and came home after midsummer. That he called spring-viking. Then he was at home until the corn- fields were reaped down, and the grain seen to and stored. Then he fared away on a viking-voyage, and then he did not come home till the winter was one month off, and that he called his au- tumn- viking." (6)

Toward the end of the ninth century Harold Fairhair, either spurred by the example of Charlemagne, or really prompted, as Snorri Sturluson tells us, resolved to bring all Norway under him. As Snorri has it in "Heimskringla": "King Harold sent his men to a girl hight Gyda.... The king wanted her for his leman; for she was wondrous beautiful but of high mood withal. Now when the messengers came there and gave their message to her, she made answer that she would not throw herself away even to take a king for her husband, who swayed no greater kingdom than a few districts; `And methinks,' said she, `it is a marvel that no king here in Norway will put all the land under him, after the fashion that Gorm the Old did in Denmark, or Eric at Upsala.' The messengers deemed this a dreadfully proud-spoken answer, and asked her what she thought would come of such an one, for Harold was so mighty a man that his asking was good enough for her. But although she had replied to their saying otherwise than they would, they saw no likelihood, for this while, of bearing her along with them against her will, so they made ready to fare back again. When they were ready and the folk followed them out, Gyda said to the messengers -- `Now tell to King Harold these my words: -- I will only agree to be his lawful wife upon the condition that he shall first, for sake of me, put under him the whole of Norway, so that he may bear sway over that kingdom as freely and fully as King Eric over the realm of Sweden, or King Gorm over Denmark; for only then, methinks, can he be called king of a people.' Now his men came back to King Harold, bringing him the words of the girl, and saying she was so bold and heedless that she well deserved the king should send a greater troop of people for her, and put her to some disgrace. Then answered the king. `This maid has not spoken or done so much amiss that she should be punished, but the rather should she be thanked for her words. She has reminded me,' said he, `of somewhat that it seems wonderful I did not think of before. And now,' added he, `I make the solemn vow, and take who made me and rules over all things, to witness that never shall I clip or comb my hair until I have subdued all Norway with scatt, and duties, and lordships; or, if not, have died in the seeking.' Guttorm gave great thanks to the king for his oath, saying it was "royal work fulfilling royal rede." The new and strange government that Harold tried to enforce -- nothing less than the feudal system in a rough guise - -- which made those who had hitherto been their own men save at special times, the king's men at all times, and laid freemen under tax, was withstood as long as might be by the sturdy Norsemen. It was only by dint of hard fighting that he slowly won his way, until at Hafrsfirth he finally crushed all effective opposition. But the discontented, "and they were a great multitude," fled oversea to the outlands, Iceland, the Faroes, the Orkneys, and Ireland. The whole coast of Europe, even to Greece and the shores of the Black Sea, the northern shores of Africa, and the western part of Asia, felt the effects also. Rolf Pad-th'-hoof, son of Harold's dear friend Rognvald, made an outlaw for a cattle-raid within the bounds of the kingdom, betook himself to France, and, with his men, founded a new people and a dynasty.

Iceland had been known for a good many years, but its only dwellers had been Irish Culdees, who sought that lonely land to pray in peace. Now, however, both from Norway and the Western Isles settlers began to come in. Aud, widow of Olaf the White, King of Dublin, came, bringing with her many of mixed blood, for the Gaedhil (pronounced "Gael", Irish) and the Gaill (pronounced "Gaul", strangers) not only fought furiously, but made friends firmly, and often intermarried. Indeed, the Westmen were among the first arrivals, and took the best parts of the island -- on its western shore, appropriately enough. After a time the Vikings who had settled in the Isles so worried Harold and his kingdom, upon which they swooped every other while, that he drew together a mighty force, and fell upon them wheresoever he could find them, and followed them up with fire and sword; and this he did twice, so that in those lands none could abide but folk who were content to be his men, however lightly they might hold their allegiance. Hence it was to Iceland that all turned who held to the old ways, and for over sixty years from the first comer there was a stream of hardy men pouring in, with their families and their belongings, simple yeomen, great and warwise chieftains, rich landowners, who had left their land "for the overbearing of King Harold," as the "Landnamabok" (7) has it. "There also we shall escape the troubling of kings and scoundrels", says the

"Vatsdaelasaga". So much of the best blood left Norway that the king tried to stay the leak by fines and punishments, but in vain.

As his ship neared the shore, the new-coming chief would leave it to the gods as to where he settled. The hallowed pillars of the high seat, which were carried away from his old abode, were thrown overboard, with certain rites, and were let drive with wind and wave until they came ashore. The piece of land which lay next the beach they were flung upon was then viewed from the nearest hill-summit, and place of the homestead picked out. Then the land was hallowed by being en-circled with fire, parcelled among the band, and marked out with boundary-signs; the houses were built, the "town" or home-field walled in, a temple put up, and the settlement soon assumed shape. In 1100 there were 4500 franklins, making a population of about 50,000, fully three- fourths of whom had a strong infusion of Celtic blood in them. The mode of life was, and is, rather pastoral than aught else. In the 39,200 square miles of the island's area there are now about 250 acres of cul-tivated land, and although there has been much more in times past, the Icelanders have always been forced to reckon upon flocks and herds as their chief resources, grain of all kinds, even rye, only growing in a few favoured places, and very rarely there; the hay, self-sown, being the only certain harvest. On the coast fishing and fowling were of help, but nine-tenths of the folk lived by their sheep and cattle. Potatoes, carrots, turnips, and several kinds of cabbage have, however, been lately grown with success. They produced their own food and clothing, and could ex-port enough wool, cloth, horn, dried fish, etc., as enabled them to obtain wood for building, iron for tools, honey, wine, grain, etc, to the extent of their simple needs. Life and work was lotted by the seasons and their changes; outdoor work -- fishing, herding, hay-making, and fuel- getting -- filling the long days of summer, while the long, dark winter was used in weaving and a hundred indoor crafts. The climate is not so bad as might be expected, seeing that the island touches the polar circle, the mean temperature at Reykjavik being 39 degrees.

The religion which the settlers took with them into Iceland -- the ethnic reli-gion of the Norsefolk, which fought its last great fight at Sticklestead, where Olaf Haraldsson lost his life and won the name of Saint -- was, like all religions, a com-pound of myths, those which had survived from savage days, and those which ex-pressed the various degrees of a growing knowledge of life and better understanding of nature. Some historians and commentators are still fond of the unscientific method of taking a later religion, in this case christianity, and writing down all apparently coincident parts of belief, as having been borrowed from the christian teachings by the Norsefolk, while all that remain they lump under some slighting head. Every folk has from the beginning of time sought to explain the wonders of nature, and has, after its own fashion, set forth the mysteries of life. The lowest savage, no less than his more advanced brother, has a philosophy of the universe by which he solves the world-problem to his own satisfaction, and seeks to reconcile his conduct with his conception of the nature of things. Now, it is not to be thought, save by "a priori" reasoners, that such a folk as the Northmen -- a mighty folk, far advanced in the arts of life, imaginative, literary -- should have had no further creed than the totemistic myths of their primitive state; a state they have wholly left ere they enter history. Judging from universal analogy, the religion of which record remains to us was just what might be looked for at the particular stage of advancement the Northmen had reached. Of course something may have been gained from contact with other peoples -- from the Greeks during the long years in which the northern races pressed upon their frontier; from the Irish during the existence of the western viking-kingdoms; but what I particularly warn young students against is the constant effort of a certain order of minds to wrest facts into agreement with their pet theories of religion or what not. The whole tendency of the more modern investigation shows that the period of myth-transmission is long over ere history begins. The same confusion of different stages of myth- making is to be found in the Greek religion, and indeed in those of all peoples; similar conditions of mind produce similar practices, apart from all borrowing of ideas and manners; in Greece we find snake-dances, bear-dances, swimming with sacred pigs, leaping about in imitation of wolves, dog-feasts, and offering of dogs' flesh to the gods -- all of them practices dating from crude savagery, mingled with ideas of exalted and noble beauty, but none now, save a bigot, would think of accusing the Greeks of having stolen all their higher beliefs. Even were some part of the matter of their myths taken from others, yet the Norsemen have given their gods a noble, upright, great spirit, and placed them upon a high level that is all their own. (8) From the prose Edda the following all too brief statement of the salient points of Norse belief is made up: -- "The first and eldest of gods is hight Allfather; he lives

from all ages, and rules over all his realm, and sways all things great and small; he
smithied heaven and earth, and the lift, and all that belongs to them; what is most,
he made man, and gave him a soul that shall live and never perish; and all men that
are right-minded shall live and be with himself in Vingolf; but wicked men fare to
Hell, and thence into Niithell, that is beneath in the ninth world. Before the earth
`'twas the morning of time, when yet naught was, nor sand nor sea was there, nor
cooling streams. Earth was not found, nor Heaven above; a Yawning-gap there was,
but grass nowhere.' Many ages ere the earth was shapen was Niflheim made, but
first was that land in the southern sphere hight Muspell, that burns and blazes, and
may not be trodden by those who are outlandish and have no heritage there. Surtr
sits on the border to guard the land; at the end of the world he will fare forth, and
harry and overcome all the gods and burn the world with fire. Ere the races were
yet mingled, or the folk of men grew, Yawning-gap, which looked towards the
north parts, was filled with thick and heavy ice and rime, and everywhere within
were fog and gusts; but the south side of Yawning-gap lightened by the sparks and
gledes that flew out of Muspell-heim; as cold arose out of Niflheim and all things
grim, so was that part that looked towards Muspell hot and bright; but Yawning-
gap was as light as windless air, and when the blast of heat met the rime, so that it
melted and dropped and quickened; from those life- drops there was shaped the
likeness of a man, and he was named Ymir; he was bad, and all his kind; and so it is
said, when he slept he fell into a sweat; then waxed under his left hand a man and
a woman, and one of his feet got a son with the other, and thence cometh the
Hrimthursar. The next thing when the rime dropped was that the cow hight Aud-
humla was made of it; but four milk-rivers ran out of her teats, and she fed Ymir;
she licked rime-stones that were salt, and the first day there came at even, out of the
stones, a man's hair, the second day a man's head, the third day all the man was
there. He is named Turi; he was fair of face, great and mighty; he gat a son named
Bor, who took to him Besla, daughter of Bolthorn, the giant, and they had three
sons, Odin, Vili, and Ve. Bor's sons slew Ymir the giant, but when he fell there ran
so much blood out of his wounds that all the kin of the Hrimthursar were drowned,
save Hvergelmir and his household, who got away in a boat. Then Bor's sons took
Ymir and bore him into the midst of Yawning-gap, and made of him the earth; of
his blood seas and waters, of his flesh earth was made; they set the earth fast, and

laid the sea round about it in a ring without; of his bones were made rocks; stones and pebbles of his teeth and jaws and the bones that were broken; they took his skull and made the lift thereof, and set it up over the earth with four sides, and under each corner they set dwarfs, and they took his brain and cast it aloft, and made clouds. They took the sparks and gledes that went loose, and had been cast out of Muspellheim, and set them in the lift to give light; they gave resting-places to all fires, and set some in the lift; some fared free under it, and they gave them a place and shaped their goings. A wondrous great smithying, and deftly done. The earth is fashioned round without, and there beyond, round about it lies the deep sea; and on that sea-strand the gods gave land for an abode to the giant kind, but within on the earth made they a burg round the world against restless giants, and for this burg reared they the brows of Ymir, and called the burg Midgard. The gods went along the sea-strand and found two stocks, and shaped out of them men; the first gave soul and life, the second wit and will to move, the third face, hearing, speech, and eye-sight. They gave them clothing and names; the man Ask and the woman Embla; thence was mankind begotten, to whom an abode was given under Midgard. Then next Bor's sons made them a burg in the midst of the world, that is called Asgard; there abode the gods and their kind, and wrought thence many tidings and feats, both on earth and in the Sky. Odin, who is hight Allfather, for that he is the father of all men and sat there in his high seat, seeing over the whole world and each man's doings, and knew all things that he saw. His wife was called Frigg, and their offspring is the Asa- stock, who dwell in Asgard and the realms about it, and all that stock are known to be gods. The daughter and wife of Odin was Earth, and of her he got Thor, him followed strength and sturdiness, thereby quells he all things quick; the strongest of all gods and men, he has also three things of great price, the hammer Miolnir, the best of strength belts, and when he girds that about him waxes his god strength one-half, and his iron gloves that he may not miss for holding his hammer's haft. Balidr is Odin's second son, and of him it is good to say, he is fair and: bright in face, and hair, and body, and him all praise; he is wise and fair-spoken and mild, and that nature is in him none may withstand his doom. Tyr is daring and best of mood; there is a saw that he is tyrstrong who is before other men and never yields; he is also so wise that it is said he is tyrlearned who is wise. Bragi is famous for wisdom, and best in tongue-wit, and cunning speech, and song-craft. `And many other are there, good and great; and one, Loki, fair of face, ill in temper and fickle of mood, is called the backbiter of the Asa, and speaker of evil redes and shame of all gods and men; he has above all that craft called sleight, and cheats all in all things. Among the children of Loki are Fenris-wolf and Midgards-worm; the second lies about all the world in the deep sea, holding his tail in his teeth, though some say Thor has slain him; but Fenris-wolf is bound until the doom of the gods, when gods and men shall come to an end, and earth and heaven be burnt, when he shall slay Odin. After this the earth shoots up from the sea, and it is green and fair, and the fields bear unsown, and gods and men shall be alive again, and sit in fair halls, and talk of old tales and the tidings that happened aforetime. The head-seat, or holiest-stead, of the gods is at Yggdrasil's ash, which is of all trees best and biggest; its boughs are spread over the whole world and stand above heaven; one root of the ash is in heaven, and under the root is the right holy spring; there hold the gods doom every day; the second root is with the Hrimthursar, where before was Yawning-gap; under that root is Mimir's spring, where knowledge and wit lie hidden; thither came Allfather and begged a drink, but got it not before he left his eye in pledge; the third root is over Niflheim, and the worm Nidhogg gnaws the root beneath. A fair hall stands under the ash by the spring, and out of it come three maidens, Norns, named Has-been, Being, Will-be, who shape the lives of men; there are beside other Norns, who come to every man that is born to shape his life, and some of these are good and some evil. In the boughs of the ash sits an eagle, wise in much, and between his eyes sits the hawk Vedrfalnir; the squirrel Ratatoskr runs up and down along the ash, bearing words of hate betwixt the eagle and the worm. Those Norns who abide by the holy spring draw from it every day water, and take the clay that lies around the well, and sprinkle them up over the ash for that its boughs should not wither or rot. All those men that have fallen in the fight, and borne wounds and toil unto death, from the beginning of the world, are come to Odin in Valhall; a very great throng is there, and many more shall yet come; the flesh of the boar Soerfmnir is sodden for them every day, and he is whole again at even; and the mead they drink that flows from the teats of the she-goat Heidhrun. The meat Odin has on his board he gives to his two wolves, Geri and Freki, and he needs no meat, wine is to him both meat and drink; ravens twain sit on his shoulders, and say into his ear all tidings that they see and hear; they are called Huginn and Muninn (mind and memory); them sends he at dawn to fly over the whole world, and they come back at breakfast-tide, thereby becomes he wise in many tidings, and for this men call him Raven's-god. Every day, when they have clothed them, the heroes put on their arms and go out into the yard and fight and fell each other; that is their play, and when it looks toward mealtime, then ride they home to Valhall and sit down to drink. For murderers and men forsworn is a great hall, and a bad, and the doors look northward; it is altogether wrought of adder-backs like a wattled house, but the worms' heads turn into the house, and blow venom, so that rivers of venom run along the hall, and in those rivers must such men wade forever." There was no priest-class; every chief was priest for his own folk, offered sacrifice, performed ceremonies, and so on.

In politics the homestead, with its franklin-owner, was the unit; the "thing", or hundred-moot, the primal organisation, and the "godord", or chieftainship, its tie. The chief who had led a band of kinsmen and followers to the new country, taken possession of land, and shared it among them, became their head-ruler and priest at home, speaker and president of their Thing, and their representative in any dealings with neighbouring chiefs and their clients. He was not a feudal lord, for any franklin could change his "godord" as he liked, and the right of "judgment by peers" was in full use. At first there was no higher organisation than the local thing. A central thing, and a speaker to speak a single "law" for the whole island, was instituted in 929, and afterwards the island was divided in four quarters, each with a court, under the Al-thing. Society was divided only into two classes of men, the free and unfree, though political power was in the hands of the franklins alone; "godi" and thrall ate the same food, spoke the same tongue, wore much the same clothes, and were nearly alike in life and habits. Among the free men there was equality in all but wealth and the social standing that cannot be separated therefrom. The thrall was a serf rather than a slave, and could own a house, etc., of his own. In a generation or so the freeman or landless retainer, if he got a homestead of his own, was the peer of the highest in the land. During the tenth century Greenland was colonised from Iceland, and by end of the same century christianity was introduced into Iceland, but made at first little difference in arrangements of society. In the thirteenth century disputes over the power and jurisdiction of the clergy led, with other matters, to civil war, ending in submission to Norway, and the breaking down of all native great houses. Although life under the commonwealth had been rough and irregular, it had been free and varied, breeding heroes and men of mark; but the "law and order" now brought in left all on a dead level of peasant proprietorship, without room for hope or opening for ambition. An alien governor ruled the island, which was divided under him into local counties, administered by sheriffs appointed by the king of Norway. The Al-thing was replaced by a royal court, the local work of the local things was taken by a subordinate of the sheriff, and things, quarter-courts, trial by jury, and all the rest, were swept away to make room for these "improvements", which have lasted with few changes into this century. In 1380 the island passed under the rule of Denmark, and so continues. (9) During the fifteenth century the English trade was the only link between Iceland and the outer world; the Danish government weakened that link as much as it could, and sought to shut in and monopolise everything Icelandic; under the deadening effect of such rule it is no marvel that everything found a lower level, and many things went out of existence for lack of use. In the sixteenth century there is little to record but the Reformation, which did little good, if any, and the ravages of English, Gascon, and Algerine pirates who made havoc on the coast; (10) they appear toward the close of the century and disappear early in the seventeenth. In the eighteenth century small-pox, sheep disease, famine, and the terrible eruptions of 1765 and 1783, follow one another swiftly and with terrible effect. At the beginning of the present century Iceland, however, began to shake off the stupor her ill-hap had brought upon her, and as European attention had been drawn to her, she was listened to. Newspapers, periodicals, and a Useful Knowledge Society were started; then came free trade, and the "home-rule" struggle, which met with partial success in 1874, and is still being carried on. A colony, Gimli, in far-off Canada, has been formed of Icelandic emigrants, and large numbers have left their mother- land; but there are many co-operative societies organised now, which it is hoped will be able to so revive the old resources of the island as to make provision for the old population and ways of life. There is now again a representative central council, but very many of the old rights and powers have not been yet restored. The condition of society is peculiar absence of towns, social equality, no abject poverty or great wealth, rarity of crime, making it easy for the whole country to be administered as a co-operative commonwealth without the great and striking changes rendered necessary by more complicated systems.

Iceland. has always borne a high name for learning and literature; on both sides of their descent people inherited special poetic power. Some of older Eddaic fragments attest the great reach and deep overpowering strength of imagination possessed by their Norse ancestors; and they themselves had been quickened by a new leaven. During the first generations of the "land-taking" a great school of poetry which had arisen among the Norsemen of the Western Isles was brought by them to Iceland. (11) The poems then produced are quite beyond parallel with those of any Teutonic language for centuries after their date, which lay between the beginning of the ninth and the end of the tenth centuries. Through the Greenland colony also came two, or perhaps more, great poems of this western school. This school grew out of the stress and storm of the viking life, with its wild adventure and varied commerce, and the close contact with an artistic and inventive folk, possessed of high culture and great learning. The infusion of Celtic blood, however slight it may have been, had also something to do with the swift intense feeling and rapidity of passion of the earlier Icelandic poets. They are hot-headed and hot-hearted, warm, impulsive, quick to quarrel or to love, faithful, brave; ready with sword or song to battle with all comers, or to seek adventure wheresoever it might be found. They leave Iceland young, and wander at their will to different courts of northern Europe, where they are always held in high honour. Gunnlaug Worm-tongue (12) in 1004 carne to England, after being in Norway, as the saga says: -- "Now sail Gunnlaug and his fellows into the English main, and come at autumntide south to London Bridge, where they hauled ashore their ship. Now, at that time King Ethelred, the son of Edgar, ruled over England, and was a good lord; the winter he sat in London. But in those days there was the same tongue in England as in Norway and Denmark; but the tongues changed when William the Bastard won England, for thenceforward French went current there, for he was of French kin. Gunnlaug went presently to the king, and greeted him well and worthily. The king asked him from what land he came, and Gunnlaug told him all as it was. `But,' said he, `I have come to meet thee, lord, for that I have made a song on thee, and I would that it might please thee to hearken to that song.' The king said it should be so, and Gunnlaug gave forth the song well and proudly, and this is the burden thereof --

"'As God are all folk fearing

The fire lord King of England,
Kin of all kings and all folk,
To Ethelred the head bow.'

The king thanked him for the song, and gave him as song-reward a scarlet cloak lined with the costliest of furs, and golden- broidered down to the hem; and made him his man; and Gunnlaug was with him all the winter, and was well accounted of."

The poems in this volume are part of the wonderful fragments which are all that remain of ancient Scandinavian poetry. Every piece which survives has been garnered by Vigfusson and Powell in the volumes of their "Corpus", where those who seek may find. A long and illustrious line of poets kept the old traditions, down even to within a couple centuries, but the earlier great harvest of song was never again equalled. After christianity had entered Iceland, and that, with other causes, had quieted men's lives, although the poetry which stood to the folk in lieu of music did not die away, it lost the exclusive hold it had upon men's minds. In a time not so stirring, when emotion was not so fervent or so swift, when there was less to quicken the blood, the story that had before found no fit expression but in verse, could stretch its limbs, as it were, and be told in prose. Something of Irish influence is again felt in this new departure and that marvellous new growth, the saga, that came from it, but is little more than an influence. Every people find some one means of expression which more than all else suits their mood or their powers, and this the Icelanders found in the saga. This was the life of a hero told in prose, but in set form, after a regular fashion that unconsciously complied with all epical requirements but that of verse -- simple plot, events in order of time, set phrases for even the shifting emotion or changeful fortune of a fight or storm, and careful avoidance of digression, comment, or putting forward by the narrator of ought but the theme he has in hand; he himself is never seen. Something in the perfection of the saga is to be traced to the long winter's evenings, when the whole household, gathered together at their spinning, weaving, and so on, would listen to one of their number who told anew some old story of adventure or achievement. In very truth the saga is a prose epic, and marked by every quality an epic should possess. Growing up while the deeds of dead heroes were fresh in memory, most often recited before the sharers in such deeds, the saga, in its pure form, never goes from what is truth to its teller. Where the saga, as this one of the Volsungs is founded upon the debris of songs and poems, even then very old, tales of mythological heroes, of men quite removed from the personal knowledge of the narrator, yet the story is so inwound with the tradition of his race, is so much a part of his thought-life, that every actor in it has for him a real existence. At the feast or gathering, or by the fireside, as men made nets and women spun, these tales were told over; in their frequent repetition by men who believed them, though incident or sequence underwent no change, they would become closer knit, more coherent, and each an organic whole. Gradually they would take a regular and accepted form, which would ease the strain upon the reciter's memory and leave his mind free to adorn the story with fair devices, that again gave help in the making it easier to remember, and thus aided in its preservation. After a couple of generations had rounded and polished the sagas by their telling and retelling, they were written down for the most part between 1141 and 1220, and so much was their form impressed upon the mind of the folk, that when learned and literary works appeared, they were written in the same style; hence we have histories alike of kingdoms, or families, or miracles, lives of saints, kings, or bishops in saga-form, as well as subjects that seem at first sight even less hopeful. All sagas that have yet appeared in English may be found in the book-list at end of this volume, but they are not a tithe of those that remain.

Of all the stories kept in being by the saga-tellers and left for our delight, there is none that so epitomises human experience; has within the same space so much of nature and of life; so fully the temper and genius of the Northern folk, as that of the Volsungs and Niblungs, which has in varied shapes entered into the literature of many lands. In the beginning there is no doubt that the story belonged to the common ancestral folk of all the Teutonic of Scando-Gothic peoples in the earliest days of their wanderings. Whether they came from the Hindu Kush, or originated in Northern Europe, brought it with them from Asia, or evolved it among the mountains and rivers it has taken for scenery, none know nor can; but each branch of their descendants has it in one form or another, and as the Icelanders were the very crown and flower of the northern folk, so also the story which is the peculiar heritage of that folk received in their hands its highest expression and most noble form. The oldest shape in which we have it is in the Eddaic poems, some of which date from unnumbered generations before the time to which most of them are usually ascribed, the time of the viking-kingdoms in the Western Isles. In these poems the only historical name is that of Attila, the great Hun leader, who filled so large a part of the imagination of the people whose power he had broken. There is no doubt that, in the days when the kingdoms of the Scando-Goths reached from the North Cape to the Caspian, that some earlier great king performed his part; but, after the striking career of Attila, he became the recognised type of a powerful foreign potentate. All the other actors are mythic-heroic. Of the Eddaic songs only fragments now remain, but ere they perished there arose from them a saga, that now given to the readers of this. The so-called Anglo-Saxons brought part of the story to England in "Beowulf"; in which also appear some incidents that are again given in the Icelandic saga of "Grettir the Strong". Most widely known is the form taken by the story in the hands of an unknown medieval German poet, who, from the broken ballads then surviving wrote the "Nibelungenlied" or more properly "Nibelungen Not" ("The Need of the Niblungs"). In this the characters are all renamed, some being more or less historical actors in mid-European history, as Theodoric of the East-Goths, for instance. The whole of the earlier part of the story has disappeared, and though Siegfried (Sigurd) has slain a dragon, there is nothing to connect it with the fate that follows the treasure; Andvari, the Volsungs, Fafnir, and Regin are all forgotten; the mythological features have become faint, and the general air of the whole is that of medieval romance. The swoard Gram is replaced by Balmung, and the Helm of Awing by the Tarn-cap -- the former with no gain, the latter with great loss. The curse of Andvari, which in the saga is grimly real, working itself out with slow, sure steps that no power of god or man can turn aside, in the medieval poem is but a mere scenic effect, a strain of mystery and magic, that runs through the changes of the story with much added picturesqueness, but that has no obvious relation to the working-out of the plot, or fulfilment of their destiny by the different characters. Brynhild loses a great deal, and is a poor creature when compared with herself in the saga; Grimhild and her fateful drink have gone; Gudrun (Chriemhild) is much more complex, but not more tragic; one new character, Rudiger, appears as the type of chivalry; but Sigurd (Siegfred) the central figure, though he has lost by the omission of so much of his life, is, as before, the embodiment of all the virtues that were dear to northern hearts. Brave, strong, generous, dignified, and utterly truthful, he moves amid a tangle of tragic events, overmastered by a mighty fate, and in life or death is still a hero without stain or flaw. It is no wonder that he survives to this day in the national songs of the Faroe Islands and in the folk-ballads of Denmark; that his legend should have been mingled with northern history through Ragnar Lodbrog, or southern through Attila and Theodoric; that it should have inspired William Morris in producing the one great English epic of the century; (13) and Richard Wagner in the mightiest among his music-dramas. Of the story as told in the saga there is no need here to speak, for to read it, as may be done a few pages farther on, is that not better than to read about it? But it may be urged upon those that are pleased and moved by the passion and power, the strength and deep truth of it, to find out more than they now know of the folk among whom it grew, and the land in which they dwelt. In so doing they will come to see how needful are a few lessons from the healthy life and speech of those days, to be applied in the bettering of our own.

H. HALLIDAY SPARLiNG.

ENDNOTES:
(1) Viking (Ice. "Vikingr"; "vik", a bay or creek, "ingr", beloning to, (or men of) freebooters.
(2) "West over the Sea" is the word for the British Isles.
(3) See Todd (J. H.). "War of the Gaedhil with the Gaill".
(4) He was son of Ingiald, son of Thora, daughter of Sigurd Snake-I'-th'-eye, son of Ragnar Lodbrok by Aslaug, daughter of Sigurd by Brynhild. The genealogy is, doubtless, quite mythical.
(5) A Collection of Sagas and other Historical Documents relating to the Settlements and Descents of the Northmen on the British Isles. Ed., G. W. Dasent, D.C.L, and Gudbrand Vigfusson, M.A. "In the Press. Longmans, London. 8vo.
(6) "Orkneyinga Saga".
(7) Landtaking-book -- "landnam", landtaking, from "at nema land", hence also the early settlers were called "landnamsmenn".
(8) To all interested in the subject of comparative mythology, Andrew Lang's two admirable books, "Custom and Myth" (1884, 8vo) and "Myth, Ritual, and Religion" (2 vols., crown 8vo,

1887), both published by Longmans, London, may be warmly recommended.

(9) Iceland was granted full independence from Denmark in 1944. -- DBK.

(10) These pirates are always appearing about the same time in English State papers as plundering along the coasts of the British Isles, especially Ireland.

(11) For all the old Scandinavian poetry extant in Icelandic, see "Corpus Poeticum Borealis" of Vigfusson and Powell.

(12) Snake-tongue -- so called from his biting satire.

(13) "Sigurd the Volsung", which seems to have become all but forgotten in this century. -- DBK.

TRANSLATORS' PREFACE.

In offering to the reader this translation of the most complete and dramatic form of the great Epic of the North, we lay no claim to special critical insight, nor do we care to deal at all with vexed questions, but are content to abide by existing authorities, doing our utmost to make our rendering close and accurate, and, if it might be so, at the same time, not over prosaic: it is to the lover of poetry and nature, rather than to the student, that we appeal to enjoy and wonder at this great work, now for the first time, strange to say, translated into English: this must be our excuse for speaking here, as briefly as may be, of things that will seem to the student over well known to be worth mentioning, but which may give some ease to the general reader who comes across our book.

The prose of the "Volsunga Saga" was composed probably some time in the twelfth century, from floating traditions no doubt; from songs which, now lost, were then known, at least in fragments, to the Sagaman; and finally from songs, which, written down about his time, are still existing: the greater part of these last the reader will find in this book, some inserted amongst the prose text by the original story-teller, and some by the present translators, and the remainder in the latter part of the book, put together as nearly as may be in the order of the story, and forming a metrical version of the greater portion of it.

These Songs from the Elder Edda we will now briefly compare with the prose of the Volsung Story, premising that these are the only metrical sources existing of those from which the Sagaman told his tale.

Except for the short snatch on p. 24 (1) of our translation, nothing is now left of these till we come to the episode of Helgi Hundings-bane, Sigurd's half-brother; there are two songs left relating to this, from which the prose is put together; to a certain extent they cover the same ground; but the latter half of the second is, wisely as we think, left untouched by the Sagaman, as its interest is of itself too great not to encumber the progress of the main story; for the sake of its wonderful beauty, however, we could not refrain from rendering it, and it will be found first among the metrical translations that form the second part of this book.

Of the next part of the Saga, the deaths of Sinfjotli and Sigmund, and the journey of Queen Hjordis to the court of King Alf, there is no trace left of any metrical origin; but we meet the Edda once more where Regin tells the tale of his kin to Sigurd, and where Sigurd defeats and slays the sons of Hunding: this lay is known as the "Lay of Regin".

The short chap. xvi. is abbreviated from a long poem called the "Prophecy of Gripir" (the Grifir of the Saga), where the whole story to come is told with some detail, and which certainly, if drawn out at length into the prose, would have forestalled the interest of the tale.

In the slaying of the Dragon the Saga adheres very closely to the "Lay of Fafnir"; for the insertion of the song of the birds to Sigurd the present translators are responsible.

Then comes the waking of Brynhild, and her wise redes to Sigurd, taken from the Lay of Sigrdrifa, the greater part of which, in its metrical form, is inserted by the Sagaman into his prose; but the stanza relating Brynhild's awaking we have inserted into the text; the latter part, omitted in the prose, we have translated for the second part of our book.

Of Sigurd at Hlymdale, of Gudrun's dream, the magic potion of Grimhild, the wedding of Sigurd consequent on that potion; of the wooing of Brynhild for Gunnar, her marriage to him, of the quarrel of the Queens, the brooding grief and wrath of Brynhild, and the interview of Sigurd with her -- of all this, the most dramatic and best-considered parts of the tale, there is now no more left that retains its metrical form than the few snatches preserved by the Sagaman, though many of the incidents are alluded to in other poems.

Chap. xxx. is met by the poem called the "Short Lay of Sigurd", which, fragmentary apparently at the beginning, gives us something of Brynhild's awakening wrath and jealousy, the slaying of Sigurd, and the death of Brynhild herself; this poem we have translated entire.

The Fragments of the "Lay of Brynhild" are what is left of a poem partly covering the same ground as this last, but giving a different account of Sigurd's slaying; it is very incomplete, though the Sagaman has drawn some incidents from it; the reader will find it translated in our second part.

But before the death of the heroine we have inserted entire into the text as chap. xxxi. the "First Lay of Gudrun", the most lyrical, the most complete, and the most beautiful of all the Eddaic poems; a poem that any age or language might count among its most precious possessions.

From this point to the end of the Saga it keeps closely to the Songs of Edda; in chap. xxxii. the Sagaman has rendered into prose the "Ancient Lay of Gudrun", except for the beginning, which gives again another account of the death of Sigurd: this lay also we have translated.

The grand poem, called the "Hell-ride of Brynhild", is not represented directly by anything in the prose except that the Sagaman has supplied from it a link or two wanting in the "Lay of Sigrdrifa"; it will be found translated in our second part.

The betrayal and slaughter of the Giukings or Niblungs, and the fearful end of Atli and his sons, and court, are recounted in two lays, called the "Lays of Atli"; the longest of these, the "Greenland Lay of Atli", is followed closely by the Sagaman; the Shorter one we have translated.

The end of Gudrun, of her daughter by Sigurd and of her sons by her last husband Jonakr, treated of in the last four chapters of the Saga, are very grandly and poetically given in the songs called the "Whetting of Gudrun", and the "Lay of Hamdir", which are also among our translations.

These are all the songs of the Edda which the Sagaman has dealt with; but one other, the "Lament of Oddrun", we have translated on account of its intrinsic merit.

As to the literary quality of this work we in say much, but we think we may well trust the reader of poetic insight to break through whatever entanglement of strange manners or unused element may at first trouble him, and to meet the nature and beauty with which it is filled: we cannot doubt that such a reader will be intensely touched by finding, amidst all its wildness and remoteness, such a startling realism, such subtilty, such close sympathy with all the passions that may move himself to-day.

In conclusion, we must again say how strange it seems to us, that this Volsung Tale, which is in fact an unversified poem, should never before been translated into English. For this is the Great Story of the North, which should be to all our race what the Tale of Troy was to the Greeks -- to all our race first, and afterwards, when the change of the world has made our race nothing more than a name of what has been -- a story too -- then should it be to those that come after us no less than the Tale of Troy has been to us.

WILLIAM MORRIS and EIRIKR MAGNUSSON.

ENDNOTES: (1) Chapter viii. -- DBK.

THE STORY OF THE VOLSUNGS AND NIBLUNGS.
CHAPTER I.   Of Sigi, the Son of Odin.

Here begins the tale, and tells of a man who was named Sigi, and called of men the son of Odin; another man withal is told of in the tale, hight Skadi, a great man and mighty of his hands; yet was Sigi the mightier and the higher of kin, according to the speech of men of that time. Now Skadi had a thrall with whom the story must deal somewhat, Bredi by name, who was called after that work which he had to do; in prowess and might of hand he was equal to men who were held more worthy, yea, and better than some thereof.

Now it is to be told that, on a time, Sigi fared to the hunting of the deer, and the thrall with him; and they hunted deer day- long till the evening; and when they gathered together their prey in the evening, lo, greater and more by far was that which Bredi had slain than Sigi's prey; and this thing he much misliked, and he said that great wonder it was that a very thrall should out-do him in the hunting of deer: so he fell on him and slew him, and buried the body of him thereafter in a snow-drift.

Then he went home at evening tide and says that Bredi had ridden away from him into the wild-wood. "Soon was he out of my sight," he says, "and naught more I wot of him."

Skadi misdoubted the tale of Sigi, and deemed that this was a guile of his, and that he would have slain Bredi. So he sent men to seek for him, and to such an end came their seeking, that they found him in a certain snow-drift; then said Skadi, that men should call that snow-drift Bredi's Drift from henceforth; and thereafter have folk followed, so that in such wise they call every drift that is right great.

Thus it is well seen that Sigi has slain the thrall and murdered him; so he is given forth to be a wolf in holy places, (1) and may no more abide in the land with his father; therewith Odin bare him fellowship from the land, so long a way, that right long it was, and made no stay till he brought him to certain war- ships. So Sigi falls to lying out a-warring with the strength that his father gave him or ever they parted; and happy was he in his warring, and ever prevailed, till he brought it about that he won by his wars land and lordship at the last; and thereupon he took to him a noble wife, and became a great and mighty king, and ruled over the land of the Huns, and was the greatest of warriors. He had a son by his wife, who was called Refit, who grew up in his father's house, and soon became great of growth, and shapely.

ENDNOTES:
(1) "Wolf in holy places," a man put out of the pale of society   for crimes, an outlaw.

CHAPTER II. Of the Birth of Volsung, the Son of Rerir, who was the Son of Sigi.

Now Sigi grew old, and had many to envy him, so that at last those turned against him whom he trusted most; yea, even the brothers of his wife; for these fell on him at his unwariest, when there were few with him to withstand them, and brought so many against him, that they prevailed against him, and there fell Sigi and all his folk with him. But Rerir, his son, was not in this trouble, and he brought together so mighty a strength of his friends and the great men of the land, that he got to himself both the lands and kingdom of Sigi his father; and so now, when he deems that the feet under him stand firm in his rule, then he calls to mind that which he had against his mother's brothers, who had slain his father. So the king gathers together a mighty army, and therewith falls on his kinsmen, deeming that if he made their kinship of small account, yet none the less they had first wrought evil against him. So he wrought his will herein, in that he departed not from strife before he had slain all his father's banesmen, though dreadful the deed seemed in every wise. So now he gets land, lordship, and fee, and is become a mightier man than his father before him.

Much wealth won in war gat Rerir to himself, and wedded a wife withal, such as he deemed meet for him, and long they lived together, but had no child to take the heritage after them; and ill-content they both were with that, and prayed the Gods with heart and soul that they might get them a child. And so it is said that Odin hears their prayer, and Freyia no less hearkens wherewith they prayed unto her: so she, never lacking for all good counsel, calls to her her casket-bearing may, (1) the daughter of Hrimnir the giant, and sets an apple in her hand, and bids her bring it to the king. She took the apple, and did on her the gear of a crow, and went flying till she came whereas the king sat on a mound, and there she let the apple fall into the lap of the king; but he took the apple and deemed he knew whereto it would avail; so he goes home from the mound to his own folk, and came to the queen, and some deal of that apple she ate.

So, as the tale tells, the queen soon knew that she big with child, but a long time wore or ever she might give birth to the child: so it befell that the king must needs go to the wars, after the custom of kings, that he may keep his own land in peace: and in this journey it came to pass that Rerir fell sick and got his death, being minded to go home to Odin, a thing much desired of many folk in those days.

Now no otherwise it goes with the queen's sickness than heretofore, nor may she be the lighter of her child, and six winters wore away with the sickness still heavy on her; so that at the last she feels that she may not live long; wherefore now she bade cut the child from out of her; and it was done even as she bade; a man-child was it, and great of growth from his birth, as might well be; and they say that the youngling kissed his mother or ever she died; but to him is a name given, and he is called Volsung; and he was king over Hunland in the room of his father. From his early years he was big and strong, and full of daring in all manly deeds and trials, and he became the greatest of warriors, and of good hap in all the battles of his warfaring.

Now when he was fully come to man's estate, Hrimnir the giant sends to him Ljod his daughter; she of whom the tale told, that she brought the apple to Rerir, Volsung's father. So Volsung weds her withal; and long they abode together with good hap and great love. They had ten sons and one daughter, and their eldest son was hight Sigmund, and their daughter Signy; and these two were twins, and in all wise the foremost and the fairest of the children of Volsung the king, and mighty, as all his seed was; even as has been long told from ancient days, and in tales of long ago, with the greatest fame of all men, how that the Volsungs have been great men and high-minded and far above the most of men both in cunning and in prowess and all things high and mighty.

So says the story that king Volsung let build a noble hall in such a wise, that a big oak-tree stood therein, and that the limbs of the tree blossomed fair out over the roof of the hall, while below stood the trunk within it, and the said trunk did men call Branstock.

ENDNOTES:
(1) May (A.S. "maeg"), a maid.

CHAPTER III. Of the Sword that Sigmund, Volsung's son, drew from the Branstock.

There was a king called Siggeir, who ruled over Gothland, a mighty king and of many folk; he went to meet Volsung, the king, and prayed him for Signy his daughter to wife; and the king took his talk well, and his sons withal, but she was loth thereto, yet she bade her father rule in this as in all other things that concerned her, so the king took such rede (1) that he gave her to him, and she was betrothed to King Siggeir; and for the fulfilling of the feast and the wedding, was King Siggeir to come to the house of King Volsung. The king got ready the feast according to his best might, and when all things were ready, came the king's guests and King Siggeir withal at the day appointed, and many a man of great account had Siggeir with him.

The tale tells that great fires were made endlong the hall, and the great tree aforesaid stood midmost thereof, withal folk say that, whenas men sat by the fires in the evening, a certain man came into the hall unknown of aspect to all men; and suchlike array he had, that over him was a spotted cloak, and he was bare- foot, and had linen-breeches knit tight even unto the bone, and he had a sword in his hand as he went up to the Branstock, and a slouched hat upon his head: huge he was, and seeming-ancient, and one-eyed. (2) So he drew his sword and smote it into the tree- trunk so that it sank in up to the hilts; and all held back from greeting the man. Then he took up the word, and said --

"Whoso draweth this sword from this stock, shall have the same as a gift from me, and shall find in good sooth that never bare he better sword in hand than is this."

Therewith out went the old man from the hall, and none knew who he was or whither he went.

Now men stand up, and none would fain be the last to lay hand to the sword, for they deemed that he would have the best of it who might first touch it; so all the noblest went thereto first, and then the others, one after other; but none who came thereto might avail to pull it out, for in nowise would it come away howsoever they tugged at it; but now up comes Sigmund, King Volsung's son, and sets hand to the sword, and pulls it from the stock, even as if it lay loose before him; so good that weapon seemed to all, that none thought he had seen such a sword before, and Siggeir would fain buy it of him at thrice its weight of gold, but Sigmund said --

"Thou mightest have taken the sword no less than I from there whereas it stood, if it had been thy lot to bear it; but now, since it has first of all fallen into my hand, never shalt thou have it, though thou biddest therefor all the gold thou hast."

King Siggeir grew wroth at these words, and deemed Sigmund had answered him scornfully, but whereas was a wary man and a double- dealing, he made as if he heeded this matter in nowise, yet that same evening he thought how he might reward it, as was well seen afterwards.

ENDNOTES:
(1) Rede (A.S. raed), counsel, advice, a tale or prophecy.
(2) The man is Odin, who is always so represented, because he
     gave his eye as a pledge for a draught from the fountain of
     Mimir, the source of all wisdom.

CHAPTER IV. How King Siggeir wedded Signy, and bade King Volsung and his son to Gothland.

Now it is to be told that Siggeir goes to bed by Signy that night, and the next morning the weather was fair; then says King Siggeir that he will not bide, lest the wind should wax, or the sea grow impassable; nor is it said that Volsung or his sons letted him herein, and that the less, because they saw that he was fain to get him gone from the feast. But now says Signy to her father --

"I have no will to go away with Seggeir, neither does my heart smile upon him, and I wot, by my fore-knowledge, and from the fetch (1) of our kin, that from this counsel will great evil fall on us if this wedding be not speedily undone."

"Speak in no such wise, daughter!" said he, "for great shame will it be to him, yea, and to us also, to break troth with him, he being sackless; (2) and in naught may we trust him, and no friendship shall we have of him, if these matters are broken off; but he will pay us back in as evil wise as he may; for that alone is seemly, to hold truly to troth given."

So King Siggeir got ready for home, and before he went from the feast he bade King Volsung, his father-in-las, come see him in Gothland, and all his sons with him whenas three months should be overpast, and to bring such following with him, as he would have, and as he deemed meet for his honour; and thereby will Siggeir the king pay back for the shortcomings of the wedding-feast, in that he would abide thereat but one night only, a thing not according to the wont of men. So King Volsung gave word to come on the day named, and the kinsmen-in-law parted, and Siggeir went home with his wife.

ENDNOTES:
(1) Fetch; wraith, or familiar spirit.
(2) Sackless (A.S. "sacu", Icel. "sok".) blameless.

CHAPTER V. Of the Slaying of King Volsung.

Now tells the tale of King Volsung and his sons that they go at the time appointed to Gothland at the bidding of King Siggeir, and put off from the land in three ships, all well manned, and have a fair voyage, and made Gothland late of an evening tide.

But that same night came Signy and called her father and brothers to a privy talk, and told them what she deemed King Siggeir was minded to do, and how that he had drawn together an army no man may meet. "And," says she, "he is minded to do guilefully by you; wherefore I bid you get ye gone back again to your own land, and gather together the mightiest power ye may, and then come back hither and avenge you; neither go ye now to your undoing, for ye shall surely fail not to fall by his wiles if ye turn not on him even as I bid you."

Then spake Volsung the king, "All people and nations shall tell of the word I spake, yet being unborn, wherein I vowed a vow that I would flee in fear from neither fire nor the sword; even so have I done hitherto, and shall I depart therefrom now I am old? Yea withal never shall the maidens mock these my sons at the games, and cry out at them that they fear death; once alone must all men need die, and from that season shall none escape; so my rede is that we flee nowhither, but do the work of our hands in as manly wise as we may; a hundred fights have I fought and whiles I had more, and whiles I had less, and yet even had I the victory, nor shall it ever be heard tell of me that I fled away or prayed for peace."

Then Signy wept right sore, and prayed that she might not go back to King Siggeir, but King Volsung answered --

"Thou shalt surely go back to thine husband, and abide with him, howsoever it fares with us."

So Signy went home, and they abode there that night but in the morning, as soon as it was day, Volsung bade his men arise and go aland and make them ready for battle; so they went aland, all of them all-armed, and had not long to wait before Siggeir fell on them with all his army, and the fiercest fight there was betwixt them; and Siggeir cried on his men to the onset all he might; and so the tale tells that King Volsung and his sons went eight times right through Siggeir's folk that day, smiting and hewing on either hand, but when they would do so even once again, King Volsung fell amidst his folk and all his men withal, saving his ten sons, for mightier was the power against them than they might withstand.

But now are all his sons taken, and laid in bonds and led away; and Signy was ware withal that her father was slain, and her brothers taken and doomed to death, that she called King Siggeir apart to talk with her, and said --

"This will I pray of thee, that thou let not slay my brothers hastily, but let them be set awhile in the stocks, for home to me comes the saw that says, "Sweet to eye while seen": but longer life I pray not for them, because I wot well that my prayer will not avail me."

Then answered Siggeir

"Surely thou art mad and witless, praying thus for more bale for thy brothers than their present slaying; yet this will I grant thee, for the better it likes me the more they must bear, and the longer their pain is or ever death come to them."

Now he let it be done even as she prayed, and a mighty beam was brought and set on the feet of those ten brethren in a certain place of the wild-wood, and there they sit day-long until night; but at midnight, as they sat in the stocks, there came on them a she-wolf from out the wood; old she was, and both great and evil of aspect; and the first thing she did was to bite one of those brethren till he died, and then she ate him up withal, and went on her way.

But the next morning Signy sent a man to the brethren, even one whom she most trusted, to wot of the tidings; and when he came back he told her that one of them was dead, and great and grievous she deemed it, if they should all fare in like wise, and yet naught might she avail them.

Soon is the tale told thereof: nine nights together came the she- wolf at midnight, and each night slew and ate up one of the brethren, until all were dead, save Sigmund only; so now, before the tenth night came, Signy sent that trusty man to Sigmund, her brother, and gave honey into his hand, bidding him do it over Sigmund's face, and set a little deal of it in his mouth; so he went to Sigmund and did as he was bidden, and then came home again; and so the next night came the she-wolf according to her wont, and would slay him and eat him even as his brothers; but now she sniffs the breeze from him, whereas he was anointed with the honey, and licks his face all over with her tongue, and then thrusts her tongue into the mouth of him. No fear he had thereof, but caught the she-wolf's tongue betwixt his teeth, and so hard she started back thereat, and pulled herself away so mightily, setting her feet against the stock that all was riven asunder; but he ever held so fast that the tongue came away by the roots, and thereof she had her bane.

But some men say that this same she-wolf was the mother of King Siggeir, who had turned herself into this likeness by troll's lore and witchcraft.

CHAPTER VI. Of how Signy sent the Children of her and Siggeir to Sigmund.

Now whenas Sigmund is loosed and the stocks are broken, he dwells in the woods and holds himself there; but Signy sends yet again to wot of the tidings, whether Sigmund were alive or no; but when those who were sent came to him, he told them all as it had betid, and how things had gone betwixt him and the wolf; so they went home and tell Signy the tidings; but she goes and finds her brother, and they take counsel in such wise as to make a house underground in the wild-wood; and so things go on a while, Signy hiding him there, and sending him such things as he needed; but King Siggeir deemed that all the Volsungs were dead.

Now Siggeir had two sons by his wife, whereof it is told that when the eldest was ten winters old, Signy sends him to Sigmund, so that he might give him help, if he would in any wise strive to avenge his father; so the youngling goes to the wood, and comes late in evening-tide to Sigmund's earth-house; and Sigmund welcomed him in seemly fashion, and said that he should make ready their bread; "But I," said he, "will go seek firewood."

Therewith he gives the meal-bag into his hands while he himself went to fetch firing; but when he came back the youngling had done naught at the bread-making. Then asks Sigmund if the bread be ready --

Says the youngling, "I durst not set hand to the meal sack, because somewhat quick lay in the meal."

Now Sigmund deemed he wotted that the lad was of no such heart as that he would be fain to have him for his fellow; and when he met his sister, Sigmund said that he had come no nigher to the aid of a man though the youngling were with him.

Then said Signy, "Take him and kill him then; for why should such an one live longer?" and even so he did.

So this winter wears, and the next winter Signy sent her next son to Sigmund; and there is no need to make a long tale thereof, for in like wise went all things, and he slew the child by the counsel of Signy.

CHAPTER VII. Of the Birth of Sinfjotli the Son of Sigmund.

So on a tide it befell as Signy sat in her bower, that there came to her a witch-wife exceeding cunning, and Signy talked with her in such wise, "Fain am I," says she, "that we should change semblances together."

She says, "Even as thou wilt then."

And so by her wiles she brought it about that they changed semblances, and now the witch-wife sits in Signy's place according to her rede, and goes to bed by the king that night, and he knows not that he has other than Signy beside him.

But the tale tells of Signy, that she fared to the earthhouse of her brother, and prayed him give her harbouring for the night; "For I have gone astray abroad in the woods, and know not whither I am going."

So he said she might abide, and that he would not refuse harbour to one lone woman, deeming that she would scarce pay back his good cheer by tale-bearing: so. she came into the house, and they sat down to meat, and his eyes were often on her, and a goodly and fair woman she seemed to him; but when they are full, then he says to her, that he is right fain that they should have but one bed that night; she nowise turned away therefrom, and so for three nights together he laid her in bed by him.

Thereafter she fared home, and found the witch-wife and bade her change semblances again, and she did so.

Now as time wears, Signy brings forth a man-child, who was named Sinfjotli, and when he grew up he was both big and strong, and fair of face, and much like unto the kin of the Volsungs, and he was hardly yet ten winters old when she sent him to Sigmund's earth-house; but this trial she had made of her other sons or ever she had sent them to Sigmund, that she had sewed gloves on to their hands through flesh and skin, and they had borne it ill and cried out thereat; and this she now did to Sinfjotli, and he changed countenance in nowise thereat. Then she flayed off the kirtle so that the skin came off with the sleeves, and said that this would be torment enough for him; but he said --

"Full little would Volsung have felt such a smart this."

So the lad came to Sigmund, and Sigmund bade him knead their meal up, while he goes to fetch firing; so he gave him the meal-sack, and then went after the wood, and by then he came back had Sinfjotli made an end of his baking. Then asked Sigmund if he had found nothing in the meal.

"I misdoubted me that there was something quick in the meal when I first fell to kneading of it, but I have kneaded it all up together, both the meal and that which was therein, whatsoever it was."

Then Sigmund laughed out, he said --

"Naught wilt thou eat of this bread to-night, for the most deadly of worms (1) hast thou kneaded up therewith."

Now Sigmund was so mighty a man that he might eat venom and have no hurt therefrom; but Sinfjotli might abide whatso venom came on the outside of him, but might neither eat nor drink thereof.

ENDNOTES:
(1) Serpents.

CHAPTER VIII. The Death of King Siggeir and of Stigny.

The tale tells that Sigmund thought Sinfjotli over young to help him to his revenge, and will first of all harden him with manly deeds; so in summertide they fare wide through the woods and slay men for their wealth; Sigmund deems him to take much after the kin of the Volsungs, though he thinks that he is Siggeir's son, and deems him to have the evil heart of his father, with the might and daring of the Volsungs; withal he must needs think him in no wise a kinsome man, for full oft would he bring Sigmund's wrongs to his memory, and prick him on to slay King Siggeir.

Now on a time as they fare abroad in the wood for the getting of wealth, they find a certain house, and two men with great gold rings asleep therein: now these twain were spell-bound skin- changers, (1) and wolf-skins were hanging up over them in the house; and every tenth day might they come out of those skins; and they were kings' sons: so Sigmund and Sinfjofli do the wolf- skins on them, and then might they nowise come out of them, though forsooth the same nature went with them as heretofore; they howled as wolves howl but both knew the meaning of that howling; they lay out in the wild-wood, and each went his way; and a word they made betwixt them, that they should risk the onset of seven men, but no more, and that he who was first to be set on should howl in wolfish wise: "Let us not depart from this," says Sigmund, "for thou art young and over-bold, and men will deem the quarry good, when they take thee."

Now each goes his way, and when they were parted, Sigmund meets certain men, and gives forth a wolf's howl; and when Sinfjotli heard it, he went straightway thereto, and slew them all, and once more they parted. But ere Sinfjotli has fared long through the woods, eleven men meet him, and he wrought in such wise that he slew them all, and was awearied therewith, and crawls under an oak, and there takes his rest. Then came Sigmund thither, and said --

"Why didst thou not call on me?"

Sinfjotli said, "I was loth to call for thy help for the slaying of eleven men."

Then Sigmund rushed at him so hard that he staggered and fell, and Sigmund bit him in the throat. Now that day they might not come out of their wolf-skins: but Sigmund lays the other on his back, and bears him home to the house, and cursed the wolf-gears and gave them to the trolls. Now on a day he saw where two weasels went and how that one bit the other in the throat, and then ran straightway into the thicket, and took up a leaf and laid in on the wound, and thereon his fellow sprang up quite and clean whole; so Sigmund went out and saw a raven flying with a blade of that same herb to him; so he took it and drew it over Sinfjotli's hurt, and he straightway sprang up as whole as though he had never been hurt. There after they went home to their earth-house, and abode there till the time came for them to put off the wolf-shapes; then they burnt them up with fire, and prayed that no more hurt might come to any one from them; but in that uncouth guise they wrought many famous deeds in the kingdom and lordship of King Siggeir.

Now when Sinfjotli was come to man's estate, Sigmund deemed he had tried him fully, and or ever a long time has gone by he turns his mind to the avenging of his father; if so it may be brought about; so on s certain day the twain get them gone from their earth-house, and come to the abode of King Siggeir late in the evening, and go into the porch before the hall, wherein were tuns of ale, and there they lie hid: now the queen is ware of them, where they are, and is fain to meet them; and when they met they took counsel and were of one mind that Volsung should be revenged that same night.

Now Signy and the king had two children of tender age, who played with a golden toy on the floor, and bowled it along the pavement of the hall, running along with it; but therewith a golden ring from off it trundles away into the place where Sigmund and Sinfjotli lay, and off runs the little one to search for the same, and beholds withal where two men axe sitting, big and grimly to look on, with overhanging helms and bright white byrnies; (2) so he runs up the hall to his father, and tells him of the sight he has seen, and thereat the king misdoubts of some guile abiding him; but Signy heard their speech, and arose and took both the children, and went out into the porch to them and said --

"Lo ye! These younglings have bewrayed you; come now therefore and slay them!"

Sigmund says, "Never will I slay thy children for telling of where I lay hid."

But Sinfjotli made little enow of it, but drew his sword and slew them both, and cast them into the hall at King 8iggeir's feet.

Then up stood the king and cried on his men to take those who had lain privily in the porch through the night. So they ran thither and would lay hands on them, but they stood on their defence well and manly, and long he remembered it who was the nighest to them; but in the end they were borne down by many men and taken, and bonds were set upon them, and they were cast into fetters wherein they sit night long.

Then the king ponders what longest and worst of deaths he shall mete out to them; and when morning came he let make a great barrow of stones and turf; and when it was done, let set a great flat stone midmost inside thereof, so that one edge was aloft, the other alow; and so great it was that it went from wall to wall, so that none might pass it.

Now he bids folk take Sigmund and Sinfjotli and set them in the barrow, on either side of the stone, for the worse for them he deemed it, that they might hear each the other's speech, and yet that neither might pass one to the other. But now, while they were covering in the barrow with the turf-slips, thither came Signy, bearing straw with her, and cast it down to Sinfjotli, and bade the thralls hide this thing from the king; they said yea thereto, and therewithal was the barrow closed in.

But when night fell, Sinfjotli said to Sigmund, "Belike we shall scarce need meat for a while, for here has the queen cast swine's flesh into the barrow, and wrapped it round about on the outer side with straw."

Therewith he handles the flesh and finds that therein was thrust Sigmund's sword; and he knew it by the hilts as mirk as it might be in the barrow, and tells Sigmund thereof, and of that were they both fain enow.

Now Sinfjotli drave the point of the sword up into the big stone, and drew it hard along, and the sword bit on the stone. With that Sigmund caught the sword by the point, and in this wise they sawed the stone between them, and let not or all the sawing was done that need be done, even as the song sings:

> "Sinfjotli sawed
> And Sigmund sawed,
> Atwain with main
> The stone was done."

Now are they both together loose in the barrow, and soon they cut both through stone and through iron, and bring themselves out thereof. Then they go home to the hall, whenas all men slept there, and bear wood to the hall, and lay fire therein; and withal the folk therein are waked by the smoke, and by the hall burning over their heads.

Then the king cries out, "Who kindled this fire, I burn withal?"

"Here am I," says Sigmund, "with Sinfjotli, my sister's son; and we are minded that thou shalt wot well that all the Volsungs are not yet dead."

Then he bade his sister come out, and take all good things at his hands, and great honour, and fair atonement in that wise, for all her griefs.

But she answered, "Take heed now, and consider, if I have kept King Siggeir in memory, and his slaying of Volsung the king! I let slay both my children, whom I deemed worthless for the revenging of our father, and I went into the wood to thee in a witch-wife's shape; and now behold, Sinfjotli is the son of thee and of me both! And therefore has he this so great hardihood and fierceness, in that he is the son both of Volsung's son and Volsung's daughter; and for this, and for naught else, have I so wrought, that Siggeir might get his bane at last; and all these things have I done that vengeance might fall on him, and that I too might not live long; and merrily now will I die with King Siggeir, though I was naught merry to wed him."

Therewith she kissed Sigmund her brother, and Sinfjotli, and went back again into the fire, and there she died with King Siggeir and all his good men.

But the two kinsmen gathered together folk and ships, and Sigmund went back to his father's land, and drave away thence the king, who had set himself down there in the room of king Volsung.

So Sigmund became a mighty King and far-famed, wise and high- minded: he had to wife one named Borghild, and two sons they had between them, one named

Helgi and the other Hamund; and when Helgi was born, Norns came to him, (3) and spake over him, and said that he should be in time to come the most renowned of all kings. Even therewith was Sigmund come home from the wars, and so therewith he gives him the name of Helgi, and these matters as tokens thereof, Land of Rings, Sun-litten Hill and Sharp-shearing Sword, and withal prayed that he might grow of great fame, and like unto the kin of the Volsungs.

And so it was that he grew up high-minded, and well beloved, and above all other men in all prowess; and the story tells that he went to the wars when he was fifteen winters old. Helgi was lord and ruler over the army, but Sinfjotli was gotten to be his fellow herein; the twain bare sway thereover.

ENDNOTES:

(1) "Skin-changers" were universally believed in once, in
       Iceland no less than elsewhere, as see Ari in several places
       of his history, especially the episode of Dufthach and
       Storwolf o' Whale. Men possessing the power of becoming
       wolves at intervals, in the present case compelled so to
       become, wer-wolves or "loupsgarou", find large place in
       medieval story, but were equally well-known in classic
       times. Belief in them still lingers in parts of Europe
       where wolves are to be found. Herodotus tells of the Neuri,
       who assumed once a year the shape of wolves; Pliny says that
       one of the family of Antaeus, chosen by lot annually, became
       a wolf, and so remained for nine years; Giraldus Cambrensis
       will have it that Irishmen may become wolves; and Nennius
       asserts point-blank that "the descendants of wolves are
       still in Ossory;" they retransform themselves into wolves
       when they bite. Apuleius, Petronius, and Lucian have
       similar stories. The Emperor Sigismund convoked a council
       of theologians in the fifteenth century who decided that
       wer-wolves did exist.
(2) Byrny (A.S. "byrne"), corslet, cuirass.
(3) "Norns came to him." Nornir are the fates of the northern
       mythology. They are three -- "Urd", the past; "Verdandi",
       the present; and "Skuld", the future. They sit beside the

fountain of Urd ("Urdarbrienur"), which is below one of the
roots of "Yggdrasil", the world-tree, which tree their
office it is to nourish by sprinkling it with the water of
the fountain.

CHAPTER IX. How Helgi, the son of Sigmund, won King Hodbrod and his Realm, and wedded Sigurn.

Now the tale tells that Helgi in his warring met a king hight Hunding, a mighty king, and lord of many men and many lands; they fell to battle together, and Helgi went forth mightily, and such was the end of that fight that Helgi had the victory, but King Hunding fell and many of his men with him; but Helgi is deemed to have grown greatly in fame because he had slain so mighty a king.

Then the sons of Hunding draw together a great army to avenge their father. Hard was the fight betwixt them; but Helgi goes through the folk of those brothers unto their banner, and there slays these sons of Hunding, Alf and Eyolf, Herward and Hagbard, and wins there a great victory.

Now as Helgi fared from the fight he met a many women right fair and worthy to look on, who rode in exceeding noble array; but one far excelled them all; then Helgi asked them the name of that their lady and queen, and she named herself Sigrun, and said she was daughter of King Hogni.

Then said Helgi, "Fare home with us: good welcome shall ye have!"

Then said the king's daughter, "Other work lies before us than to drink with thee."

"Yea, and what work, king's daughter?" said Helgi.

She answers, "King Hogni has promised me to Hodbrod, the son of King Granmar, but I have vowed a vow that I will have him to my husband no more than if he were a crow's son and not a king's; and yet will the thing come to pass, but and if thou standest in the way thereof and goest against him with an army, and takest me away withal; for verily with no king would I rather bide on bolster than with thee."

"Be of good cheer, king's daughter," says he, "for certes he and I shall try the matter, or ever thou be given to him; yea, we shall behold which may prevail against the other; and hereto I pledge my life."

Thereafter, Helgi sent men with money in their hand to summon his folk to him, and all his power is called together to Red-Berg: and there Helgi abode till such time as a great company came to him from Hedinsey; and therewithal came mighty power from Norvi Sound aboard great and fair ships. Then King Helgi called to him the captain of his ships, who was hight Leif, and asked him if he had told over the tale of his army.

"A thing not easy to tell, lord," says he, "on the ships that came out of Norvi Sound are twelve thousand men, and otherwhere are half as many again."

Then bade King Helgi turn into the firth, called Varin's firth, and they did so: but now there fell on them so fierce a storm and so huge a sea, that the beat of the waves on board and bow was to hearken to like as the clashing together of high hills broken.

But Helgi bade men fear naught, nor take in any sail, but rather hoist every rag higher than heretofore; but little did they miss of foundering or ever they made land; then came Sigrun, daughter of King Hogni, down on to the beach with a great army, and turned them away thence to a good haven called Gnipalund; but the landsmen see what has befallen and come down to the sea-shore. The brother of King Hodbrod, lord of a land called Swarin's Cairn, cried out to them, and asked them who was captain over that mighty army. Then up stands Sinfjotli, with a helm on his head, bright shining as glass, and a byrny as white as snow; a spear in his hand, and thereon a banner of renown, and a gold- rimmed shield hanging before him; and well he knew with what words to speak to kings --

"Go thou and say, when thou hast made an end of feeding thy swine and thy dogs, and when thou beholdest thy wife again, that here are come the Volsungs, and in this company may King Helgi be found, if Hodbrod be fain of finding him, for his game and his joy it is to fight and win fame, while thou art kissing the hand-maids by the fire-side."

Then answered Granmar, "In nowise knowest thou how to speak seemly things, and to tell of matters remembered from of old, whereas thou layest lies on chiefs and lords; most like it is that thou must have long been nourished with wolf-meat abroad in the wild-woods, and has slain thy brethren; and a marvel it is to behold that thou darest to join thyself to the company of good men and true, thou, who hast sucked the blood of many a cold corpse."

Sinfjotli answered, "Dim belike is grown thy memory now, of how thou wert a witch-wife on Varinsey, and wouldst fain have a man to thee, and chose me to that same office of all the world; and how thereafter thou wert a Valkyria (1) in Asgarth, and it well- nigh came to this, that for thy sweet sake should all men fight; and nine wolf whelps I begat on thy body in Lowness, and was the father to them all."

Granmar answers, "Great skill of lying hast thou; yet belike the father of naught at all mayst thou be, since thou wert gelded by the giant's daughters of Thrasness; and lo thou art the stepson of King Siggeir, and were wont to lie abroad in wilds and woods with the kin of wolves; and unlucky was the hand wherewith thou slewest thy brethren making for thyself an exceeding evil name."

Said Sinfjotli, "Mindest thou not then, when thou were stallion Grani's mare, and how I rode thee an amble on Bravoli, and that afterwards thou wert giant Golnir's goat herd?"

Granmar says, "Rather would I feed fowls with the flesh of thee than wrangle any longer with thee."

Then spake King Helgi, "Better were it for ye, and a more manly deed, to fight, rather than to speak such things as it is a shame even to hearken to; Granmar's sons are no friends of me and of mine, yet are they hardy men none the less."

So Granmar rode away to meet King Hodbrod, at a stead called Sunfells, and the horses of the twain were named Sveipud and Sveggjud. The brothers met in the castle-porch, and Granmar told Hodbrod of the war-news. King Hodbrod was clad in a byrny, and had his helm on his head; he asked --

"What men are anigh, why look ye so wrathful?"

Granmar says, "Here are come the Volsungs, and twelve thousand men of them are afloat off the coast, and seven thousand are at the island called Sok, but at the stead called Grindur is the greatest company of all, and now I deem withal that Helgi and his fellowship have good will to give battle."

Then said the king, "Let us send a message through all our realm, and go against them, neither let any who is fain of fight sit idle at home; let us send word to the sons of Ring, and to King Hogni, and to Alf the Old, for they are mighty warriors."

So the hosts met at Wolfstone, and fierce fight befell there; Helgi rushed forth through the host of his foes, and many a man fell there; at last folk saw a great company of shield-maidens, like burning flames to look on, and there was come Sigrun, the king's daughter. Then King Helgi fell on King Hodbrod, and smote him, and slew him even under his very banner; and Sigrun cried out --

"Have thou thanks for thy so manly deed! Now shall we share the land between us, and a day of great good hap this is to me, and for this deed shalt thou get honour and renown, in that thou hast felled to earth so mighty a king."

So Helgi took to him that realm and dwelt there long, when he had wedded Sigrun, and became a king of great honour and renown, though he has naught more to do with this story.

ENDNOTES:

(1) Valkyrja, "Chooser of the elected." The women were so
     called whom Odin sent to choose those for death in battle
     who were to join the "Einherjar" in the hall of the elected,
     "Val-holl."

CHAPTER X. The ending of Sinfjatli, Sigmund's Son.

Now the Volsungs fare back home, and have gained great renown by these deeds. But Sinfjotli betook himself to warfare anew; and therewith he had sight of an exceeding fair woman, and yearned above all things for her, but that same woman was wooed also of the brother of Borghild, the king's wife: and this matter they fought out betwixt them, and Sinfjotli slew that king; and thereafter he harried far and wide, and had many a battle and even gained the day; and he became hereby honoured and renowned above all men; but in autumn tide he came home with many ships and abundant wealth.

Then he told his tidings to the king his father, and he again to the queen, and she for her part bids him get him gone from the realm, and made as if she would in nowise see him. But Sigmund said he would not drive him away, and offered her atonement of gold and great wealth for her brother's life, albeit he said he had never erst given weregild (1) to any for the slaying of a man, but no fame it was to uphold wrong against a woman.

So seeing she might not get her own way herein, she said, "Have thy will in this matter, O my lord, for it is seemly so to be."

And now she holds the funeral feast for her brother by the aid and counsel of the king, and makes ready all things thereœor in the best of wise, and bade thither many great men.

At that feast, Borghild the queen bare the drink to folk, and she came over against Sinfjofli with a great horn, and said --

"Fall to now and drink, fair stepson!"

Then he took the horn to him, and looked therein, and said --

"Nay, for the drink is charmed drink"

Then said Sigmund, "Give it unto me then;" and therewith he took the horn and drank it off.

But the queen said to Sinfjotli, "Why must other men needs drink thine ale for thee?" And she came again the second time with the horn, and said, "Come now and drink!" and goaded him with many words.

And he took the horn, and said --

"Guile is in the drink."

And thereon, Sigmund cried out --

"Give it then unto me!"

Again, the third time, she came to him, and bade him drink off his drink, if he had the heart of a Volsung; then he laid hand on the horn, but said --

"Venom is therein."

"Nay, let the lip strain it out then, O son," quoth Sigmund; and by then was he exceeding drunk with drink, and therefore spake he in that wise.

So Sinfjotli drank, and straightway fell down dead to the ground.

Sigmund rose up, and sorrowed nigh to death over him; then he took the corpse in his arms and fared away to the wood, and went till he came to a certain firth; and then he saw a man in a little boat; and that man asked if he would be wafted by him over the firth, and he said yes thereto; but so little was the boat, that they might not all go in it at once, so the corpse was first laid therein, while Sigmund went by the firth-side. But therewith the boat and the man therein vanished away from before Sigmund's eyes. (2)

So thereafter Sigmund turned back home, and drave away the queen, and a little after she died. But Sigmund the king yet ruled his realm, and is deemed ever the greatest champion and king of the old law.

ENDNOTES:

(1) Weregild, fine for man-slaying ("wer", man, and "gild", a
    payment).
(2) The man in the boat is Odin, doubtless.

CHAPTER XI.

Of King Sigmund's last Battle, and of how he must yield up his Sword again. There was a king called Eylimi, mighty and of great fame, and his daughter was called Hjordis, the fairest and wisest of womankind; and Sigmund hears it told of her that she was meet to be his wife, yea if none else were. So he goes to the house of King Eylimi, who would make a great feast for him, if so be he comes not thither in the guise of a foe. So messages were sent from one to the other that this present journey was a peaceful one, and not for war; so the feast was held in the best of wise and with many a man thereat; fairs were in every place established for King Sigmund, and all things else were done to the aid and comfort of his journey: so he came to the feast, and both kings hold their state in one hall; thither also was come King Lyngi, son of King Hunding, and he also is a-wooing the daughter of King Eylimi.

Now the king deemed he knew that the twain had come thither but for one errand, and thought withal that war and trouble might be looked for from the hands of him who brought not his end about; so he spake to his daughter, and said --

"Thou art a wise woman, and I have spoken it, that thou alone shalt choose a husband for thyself; choose therefore between these two kings, and my rede shall be even as thine."

"A hard and troublous matter," says she; "yet will I choose him who is of greatest fame, King Sigmund to wife albeit he is well stricken in years."

So to him was she betrothed, and King Lyngi gat him gone. Then was Sigmund wedded to Hjordis, and now each day was the feast better and more glorious than on the day before it. But thereafter Sigmund went back home to Hunland, and King Eylimi, his father-in-law, with him, and King Sigmund betakes himself to the due ruling of his realm.

But King Lyngi and his brethren gather an army together to fall on Sigmund, for as in all matters they were wont to have the worser lot, so did this bite the sorest of all; and they would fain prevail over the might and pride of the Volsungs. So they came to Hunland, and sent King Sigmund word how that they would not steal upon him and that they deemed he would scarce slink away from them. So Sigmund said he would come and meet them in battle, and drew his power together; but Hjordis was borne into the wood with a certain bondmaid, and mighty wealth went with them; and there she abode the while they fought.

Now the vikings rushed from their ships in numbers not to be borne up against, but Sigmund the King, and Eylimi set up their banners, and the horns blew up to battle; but King Sigmund let blow the horn his father erst had had, and cheered on his men to the fight, but his army was far the fewest.

Now was that battle fierce and fell, and though Sigmund were old, yet most hardily he fought, and was ever the foremost of his men; no shield or byrny might hold against him, and he went ever through the ranks of his foemen on that day, and no man might see how things would fare between them; many an arrow and many a spear was aloft in air that day, and so his spae-wrights wrought for him that he got no wound, and none can tell over the tale of those who fell before him, and both his arms were red with blood, even to the shoulders.

But now whenas the battle had dured a while, there came a man into the fight clad in a blue cloak, and with a slouched hat on his head, one-eyed he was, (1) and bare a bill in his hand; and he came against Sigmund the King, and have up his bill against him, and as Sigmund smote fiercely with the sword it fell upon the bill and burst asunder in the midst: thenceforth the slaughter and dismay turned to his side, for the good-hap of King Sigmund had departed from him, and his men fell fast about him; naught did the king spare himself, but the rather cheered on his men; but even as the saw says, "No might 'gainst many", so was it now proven; and in this fight fell Sigmund the King, and King Eylimi, his father-in-law, in the fore-front of their battle, and therewith the more part of their folk.

ENDNOTES:
  (1) Odin coming to change the ownership of the sword he had
      given Sigmund. See Chapter 3.

CHAPTER XII. Of the Shards of the Sword Gram, and how Hjordis went to King Alf.

Now King Lyngi made for the king's abode, and was minded to take the king's daughter there, but failed herein, for there he found neither wife nor wealth; so he fared through all the realm, and gave his men rule thereover, and now deemed that he had slain all the kin of the Volsungs, and that he need dread them no more from henceforth.

Now Hjordis went amidst the slain that night of the battle, and came whereas lay King Sigmund, and asked if he might be healed; but he answered --

"Many a man lives after hope has grown little; but my good-hap has departed from me, nor will I suffer myself to be healed, nor wills Odin that I should ever draw sword again, since this my sword and his is broken; lo now, I have waged war while it was his will."

"Naught ill would I deem matters," said she, "if thou mightest be healed and avenge my father."

The king said, "That is fated for another man; behold now, thou art great with a man-child; nourish him well; and with good heed, and the child shall be the noblest and most famed of all our kin: and keep well withal the shards of the sword: thereof shall a goodly sword be made, and it shall be called Gram, and our son shall bear it, and shall work many a great work therewith, even such as eld shall never minish; for his name shall abide and flourish as long as the world shall endure: and let this be enow for thee. But now I grow weary with my wounds, and I will go see our kin that have gone before me."

So Hjordis sat over him till he died at the day-dawning; and then she looked, and behold, there came many ships sailing to the land: then she spake to the hand-maid --

"Let us now change raiment, and be thou called by my name, and say that thou art the king's daughter."

And thus they did; but now the vikings behold the great slaughter of men there, and see where two women fare away thence into the wood; and they deem that some great tidings must have befallen, and they leaped ashore from out their ships. Now the captain of these folks was Alf, son of Hjalprek, king of Denmark, who was sailing with his power along the land. So they came into the field among the slain, and saw how many men lay dead there; then the king bade go seek for the women and bring them thither, and they did so. He asked them what women they were; and, little as the thing seems like to be, the bondmaid answered for the twain, telling of the fall of King Sigmund and King Eylimi, and many another great man, and who they were withal who had wrought the deed. Then the king asks if they wotted where the wealth of the king was bestowed; and then says the bondmaid --

"It may well be deemed that we know full surely thereof."

And therewith she guides them to the place where the treasure lay: and there they found exceeding great wealth; so that men deem they have never seen so many things of price heaped up together in one place. All this they bore to the ships of King Alf, and Hjordis and bondmaid went them. Therewith these sail away to their own realm, and talk how that surely on that field had fallen the most renowned of kings.

So the king sits by the tiller, but the women abide in the forecastle; but talk he had with the women and held their counsels of much account.

In such wise the king came home to his realm with great wealth, and he himself was a man exceeding goodly to look on. But when he had been but a little while at home, the queen, his mother, asked him why the fairest of the two women had the fewer rings and the less worthy attire.

"I deem," she said, "that she whom ye have held of least account is the noblest of the twain."

He answered: "I too have misdoubted me, that she is little like a bondwoman, and when we first met, in seemly wise she greeted noble men. Lo now, we will make trial of the thing."

So on a time as men sat at the drink, the king sat down to talk with the women, and said: --

"In what wise do ye note the wearing of the hours, whenas night grows old, if ye may not see the lights of heaven?"

Then says the bondwoman, "This sign have I, that whenas in my youth I was wont to drink much in the dawn, so now when I no longer use that manner, I am yet wont to wake up at that very same tide, and by that token do I know thereof."

Then the king laughed and said, "Ill manners for a king's daughter!" And therewith he turned to Hjordis, and asked her even the same question; but she answered --

"My father erst gave me a little gold ring of such nature, that it groweth cold on my finger in the day-dawning; and that is the sign that I have to know thereof."

The king answered: "Enow of gold there, where a very bondmaid bore it! But come now, thou hast been long enow hid from me; yet if thou hadst told me all from the beginning, I would have done to thee as though we had both been one king's children: but better than thy deeds will I deal with thee, for thou shalt be my wife, and due jointure will I pay thee whenas thou hast borne me a child."

She spake therewith and told out the whole truth about herself: so there was she held in great honour, and deemed the worthiest of women.

CHAPTER XIII. Of the Birth and Waxing of Sigurd Fafnir's-bane.

The tale tells that Hjordis brought forth a man-child, who was straightly borne before King Hjalprek, and then was the king glad thereof, when he saw the keen eyes in the head of him, and he said that few men would be equal to him or like unto him in any wise. So he was sprinkled with water, and had to name Sigurd, of whom all men speak with one speech and say that none was ever his like for growth and goodliness. He was brought up in the house of King Hjalprek in great love and honour; and so it is, that whenso all the noblest men and greatest kings are named in the olden tales, Sigurd is ever put before them all for might and prowess, for high mind and stout heart; wherewith he was far more abundantly gifted than any man of the northern parts of the wide world.

So Sigurd waxed in King Hjalprek's house, and there was no child but loved him; through him was Hjordis betrothed to King Alf, and jointure meted to her.

Now Sigurd's foster-father was hight Regin, the son of Hreidmar; he taught him all manner of arts, the chess play, and the lore of runes, and the talking of many tongues, even as the wont was with kings' sons in those days. But on a day when they were together, Regin asked Sigurd, if he knew how much wealth his father had owned, and who had the ward thereof; Sigurd answered, and said that the kings kept the ward thereof.

Said Regin, "Dost thou trust them all utterly?"

Sigurd said, "It is seemly that they keep it till I may do somewhat therewith, for better they wot how to guard it than I do."

Another time came Regin to talk to Sigurd, and said --

"A marvellous thing truly that thou must needs be a horse-boy to the kings, and go about like a running knave."

"Nay," said Sigurd, "it is not so, for in all things I have my will, and whatso thing I desire is granted me with good will."

"Well, then," said Regin, "ask for a horse of them."

"Yea," quoth Sigurd, "and that shall I have, whenso I have need thereof."

Thereafter Sigurd went to the king, and the king said --

"What wilt thou have of us?"

Then said Sigurd, "I would even a horse of thee for my disport."

Then said the king, "Choose for thyself a horse, and whatso thing else thou desirest among my matters."

So the next day went Sigurd to the wood, and met on the way an old man, long-bearded, that he knew not, who asked him whither away.

Sigurd said, "I am minded to choose me a horse; come thou, and counsel me thereon."

"Well then," said he, "go we and drive them to the river which is called Busil-tarn."

They did so, and drave the horses down into the deeps of the river, and all swam back to land but one horse; and that horse Sigurd chose for himself; grey he was of hue, and young of years, great of growth, and fair to look on, nor had any man yet crossed his back.

Then spake the grey-beard, "From Sleipnir's kin is this horse come, and he must be nourished heedfully, for it will be the best of all horses;" and therewithal he vanished away.

So Sigurd called the horse Grani, the best of all the horses of the world; nor was the man he met other than Odin himself.

Now yet again spake Regin to Sigurd, and said --

"Not enough is thy wealth, and I grieve right sore, that thou must needs run here and there like s churl's son; but I can tell thee where there is much wealth for the winning, and great name and honour to be won in getting of it."

Sigurd asked where that might be, and who had watch and ward over it.

Regin answered, "Fafnir is his name, and but a little way hence he lies, on the waste of Gnita-heath; and when thou comest there thou mayst well say that thou hast never seen more gold heaped together in one place, and that none might desire more treasure, though he were the most ancient and famed of all kings."

"Young am I," says Sigurd, "yet know I the fashion of this worm, and how that none durst go against him, so huge and evil is he."

Regin said, "Nay it is not so, the fashion and the growth of him is even as of other lingworms, (1) and an over great tale men make of it; and even so would thy forefathers have deemed; but thou, though thou be of the kin of the Volsungs, shalt scarce have the heart and mind of those, who are told of as the first in all deeds of fame."

Sigurd said, "Yea, belike I have little of their hardihood and prowess, but thou hast naught to do, to lay a coward's name upon me, when I am scarce out of my childish years. Why dost thou egg me on hereto so busily?"

Regin said, "Therein lies a tale which I must needs tell thee."

"Let me hear the same," said Sigurd.

ENDNOTES:

(1) Lingworm -- longworm, dragon.

CHAPTER XIV. Regin's tale of his Brothers, and of the Gold called Andvari's Hoard.

The tale begins," said Regin. "Hreidmar was my father's name, a mighty man and z wealthy: and his first son was named Fafnir, his second Otter, and I was the third, and the least of them all both for prowess and good conditions, but I was cunning to work in iron, and silver, and gold, whereof I could make matters that availed somewhat. Other skill my brother Otter followed, and had another nature withal, for he was a great fisher, and above other men herein; in that he had the likeness of an otter by day, and dwelt ever in the river, and bare fish to bank in his mouth, and his prey would he ever bring to our father, and that availed him much: for the most part he kept him in his otter-gear, and then he would come home, and eat alone, and slumbering, for on the dry land he might see naught. But Fafnir was by far the greatest and grimmest, and would have all things about called his.

"Now," says Regin, "there was a dwarf called Andvari, who ever abode in that force, (1) which was called Andvari's force, in the likeness of a pike, and got meat for himself, for many fish there were in the force; now Otter, my brother, was ever wont to enter into the force, and bring fish aland, and lay them one by one on the bank. And so it befell that Odin, Loki, and Hoenir, as they went their ways, came to Andvari's force, and Otter had taken a salmon, and ate it slumbering upon the river bank; then Loki took a stone and cast it at Otter, so that he gat his death thereby; the gods were well content with their prey, and fell to flaying off the otter's skin; and in the evening they came to Hreidmar's house, and showed him what they had taken: thereon he laid hands on them, and doomed them to such ransom, as that they should fill the otter skin with gold, and cover it over without with red gold; so they sent Loki to gather gold together for them; he came to Ran, (2) and got her

net, and went therewith to Andvari's force, and cast the net before the pike, and the
pike ran into the net and was taken. Then said Loki --

> "`What fish of all fishes,
>   Swims strong in the flood,
> But hath learnt little wit to beware?
>   Thine head must thou buy,
>   From abiding in hell,
> And find me the wan waters flame.'

"He answered --

> "`Andvari folk call me,
>   Call Oinn my father,
> Over many a force have I fared;
>   For a Norn of ill-luck,
>   This life on me lay
> Through wet ways ever to wade.'

"So Loki beheld the gold of Andvari, and when he had given up the gold, he
had but one ring left, and that also Loki took from him; then the dwarf went into a
hollow of the rocks, and cried out, that that gold-ring, yea and all the gold withal,
should be the bane of every man who should own it thereafter.

"Now the gods rode with the treasure to Hreidmar, and fulfilled the otter-skin,
and set it on its feet, and they must cover it over utterly with gold: but when this
was done then Hreidmar came forth, and beheld yet one of the muzzle hairs, and
bade them cover that withal; then Odin drew the ring, Andvari's loom, from his
hand, and covered up the hair therewith; then sang Loki --

> "`Gold enow, gold enow,
>   A great weregild, thou hast,
> That my head in good hap I may hold;
>   But thou and thy son

Are naught fated to thrive,
The bane shall it be of you both.'

"Thereafter," says Regin, "Fafnir slew his father and murdered him, nor got I aught of the treasure, and so evil he grew, that he fell to lying abroad, and begrudged any share in the wealth to any man, and so became the worst of all worms, and ever now lies brooding upon that treasure: but for me, I went to the king and became his master-smith; and thus is the tale told of how I lost the heritage of my father, and the weregild for my brother."

So spake Regin; but since that time gold is called Ottergild, and for no other cause than this.

But Sigurd answered, "Much hast thou lost, and exceeding evil have thy kinsmen been! But now, make a sword by thy craft, such a sword as that none can be made like unto it; so that I may do great deeds therewith, if my heart avail thereto, and thou wouldst have me slay this mighty dragon."

Regin says, "Trust me well herein; and with that same sword shalt thou slay Fafnir."

ENDNOTES:

(1) Waterfall (Ice. "foss", "fors").
(2) Ran is the goddess of the sea, wife of Aegir.
     The otter was
     held sacred by Norsefolk and figures in the myth and legend
     of most races besides; to this day its killing is held a
     great crime by the Parsees (Haug. "Religion of the Parsees",
     page 212). Compare penalty above with that for killing the
     Welsh king's cat ("Ancient Laws and Institutes of Wales".
     Ed., Aneurin Owen. Longman, London, 1841, 2 vols. 8vo).

CHAPTER XV.

Of the Welding together of the Shards of the Sward Gram.
So Regin makes a sword, and gives it into Sigurd's hands. He took the sword, and said --

"Behold thy smithying, Regin!" and therewith smote it into the anvil, and the sword brake; so he cast down the brand, and bade him forge a better.

Then Regin forged another sword, and brought it to Sigurd, who looked thereon.

Then said Regin, "Belike thou art well content therewith, hard master though thou be in smithying."

So Sigurd proved the sword, and brake it even as the first; then he said to Regin --

"Ah, art thou, mayhappen, a traitor and a liar like to those former kin of thine?"

Therewith he went to his mother, and she welcomed him in seemly wise, and they talked and drank together.

Then spake Sigurd, "Have I heard aright, that King Sigmund gave thee the good sword Gram in two pieces?"

"True enough," she said.

So Sigurd said, "Deliver them into my hands, for I would have them."

She said he looked like to win great fame, and gave him the sword. Therewith went Sigurd to Regin, and bade him make a good sword thereof as he best might; Regin grew wroth thereat, but went into the smithy with the pieces of the sword, thinking well meanwhile that Sigurd pushed his head far enow into the matter of smithying. So he made a sword, and as he bore it forth from the forge, it seemed to the smiths as though fire burned along the edges thereof. Now he bade Sigurd take the sword, and said he knew not how to make a sword if this one failed. Then Sigurd smote it into the anvil, and cleft it down to the stock thereof, and neither burst the sword nor brake it. Then he praised the sword much, and thereafter went to the river with a lock of wool, and threw it up against the stream, and it fell asunder when it met the sword. Then was Sigurd glad, and went home.

But Regin said, "Now whereas I have made the sword for thee, belike thou wilt hold to thy troth given, and wilt go meet Fafnir?"

"Surely will I hold thereto," said Sigurd, "yet first must I avenge my father."

Now Sigurd the older he grew, the more he grew in the love of all men, so that every child loved him well.

CHAPTER XVI. The prophecy of Grifir.

There was a man hight Grifir,(1) who was Sigurd's mother's brother, and a little after the forging of the sword Sigurd went to Grifir, because he was a man who knew things to come, and what was fated to men: of him Sigurd asked diligently how his life should go; but Grifir was long or he spake, yet at the last, by reason of Sigurd's exceeding great prayers, he told him all his life and the fate thereof, even as afterwards came to pass. So when Grifir had told him all even as he would, he went back home; and a little after he and Regin met.

Then said Regin, "Go thou and slay Fafnir, even as thou hast given thy word."

Sigurd said, "That work shall be wrought; but another is first to be done, the avenging of Sigmund the king and the other of my kinsmen who fell in that their last fight."

ENDNOTES:

(1) Called "Gripir" in the Edda.

CHAPTER XVII. Of Sigurd's Avenging of Sigmund his Father.

Now Sigurd went to the kings, and spake thus --

"Here have I abode a space with you, and I owe you thanks and reward, for great love and many gifts and all due honour; but now will I away from the land and go meet the sons of Hunding, and do them to wit that the Volsungs are not all dead; and your might would I have to strengthen me therein."

So the kings said that they would give him all things soever that he desired, and therewith was a great army got ready, and all things wrought in the most heedful wise, ships and all war-gear, so that his journey might be of the stateliest: but Sigurd himself steered the dragon-keel which was the greatest and noblest; richly wrought were their sails, and glorious to look on.

So they sail and have wind at will; but when a few days were overpast, there arose a great storm on the sea, and the waves were to behold even as the foam of men's blood; but Sigurd bade take in no sail, howsoever they might be riven, but rather to lay on higher than heretofore. But as they sailed past the rocks of a ness, a certain man hailed the ships, and asked who was captain over that navy; then was it told him that the chief and lord was Sigurd, the son of Sigmund, the most famed of all the young men who now are.

Then said the man, "Naught but one thing, certes do all say of him, that none among the sons of kings may be likened unto him; now fain were I that ye would shorten sail on some of the ships, and take me aboard."

Then they asked him of his name, and he sang --

"Hnikar I hight,

When I gladdened Huginn,
And went to battle,
Bright son of Volsung;
Now may ye call
The carl on the cliff top,
Feng or Fjolnir:
Fain would I with you."

They made for land therewith, and took that man aboard.
Then quoth Sigurd,(1) as the song says --

"Tell me this, O Hnikar,
Since full well thou knowest
Fate of Gods, good and ill of mankind,
What best our hap foresheweth,
When amid the battle
About us sweeps the sword edge."

Quoth Hnikar --

"Good are many tokens
If thereof men wotted
When the swords are sweeping:
Fair fellow deem I
The dark-winged raven,
In war, to weapon-wielder.

"The second good thing:
When abroad thou goest
For the long road well arrayed,
Good if thou seest
Two men standing,
Fain of fame within the forecourt.

"A third thing:
Good hearing,
 The wolf a howling
Abroad under ash boughs;
 Good hap shalt thou have
 Dealing with helm-staves,
If thou seest these fare before thee.

"No man in fight
His face shall turn
 Against the moon's sister
 Low, late-shining,
 For he winneth battle
 Who best beholdeth
Through the midmost sword-play,
And the sloping ranks best shapeth.

"Great is the trouble
 Of foot ill-tripping,
When arrayed for fight thou farest,
 For on both sides about
 Are the Disir (2) by thee,
Guileful, wishful of thy wounding.

"Fair-combed, well washen
 Let each warrior be,
Nor lack meat in the morning,
 For who can rule
 The eve's returning,
And base to fall before fate grovelling."

Then the storm abated, and on they fared till they came aland in the realm of

Hunding's sons, and then Fjolnir vanished away.

Then they let loose fire and sword, and slew men and burnt their abodes, and did waste all before them: a great company of folk fled before the face of them to Lyngi the King, and tell him that men of war are in the land, and are faring with such rage and fury that the like has never been heard of; and that the sons of King Hunding had no great forecast in that they said they would never fear the Volsungs more, for here was come Sigurd, the son of Sigmund, as captain over this army.

So King Lyngi let send the war-message all throughout his realm, and has no will to flee, but summons to him all such as would give him aid. So he came against Sigurd with a great army, he and his brothers with him, and an exceeding fierce fight befell; many a spear and many an arrow might men see there raised aloft, axes hard driven, shields cleft and byrnies torn, helmets were shivered, skulls split atwain, and many a man felled to the cold earth.

And now when the fight has long dured in such wise, Sigurd goes forth before the banners, and has the good sword Gram in his hand, and smites down both men and horses, and goes through the thickest of the throng with both arms red with blood to the shoulder; and folk shrank aback before him wheresoever he went, nor would either helm or byrny hold before him, and no man deemed he had ever seen his like. So a long while the battle lasted, and many a man was slain, and furious was the onset; till at last it befell, even as seldom comes to hand, when a land army falls on, that, do whatso they might, naught was brought about; but so many men fell of the sons of Hunding that the tale of them may not be told; and now whenas Sigurd was among the foremost, came the sons of Hunding against him, and Sigurd smote therewith at Lyngi the king, and clave him down, both helm and head, and mail- clad body, and thereafter he smote Hjorward his brother atwain, and then slew all the other sons of Hunding who were yet alive, and the more part of their folk withal.

Now home goes Sigurd with fair victory won, and plenteous wealth and great honour, which he had gotten to him in this journey, and feasts were made for him against he came back to the realm.

But when Sigurd had been at home but a little, came Regin to talk with him, and said --

"Belike thou wilt now have good will to bow down Fafnir's crest according to thy word plighted, since thou hast thus revenged thy father and the others of thy kin."

Sigurd answered, "That will we hold to, even as we have promised, nor did it ever fall from our memory."

ENDNOTES:

(1) This and verses following were inserted from the "Reginsmal" by the translators.
(2) "Disir", sing. "Dis". These are the guardian beings who follow a man from his birth to his death. The word originally means sister, and is used throughout the Eddaic poems as a dignified synonym for woman, lady.

CHAPTER XVIII. Of the Slaying of the Worm Fafnir.

Now Sigurd and Regin ride up the heath along that same way wherein Fafnir was wont to creep when he fared to the water; and folk say that thirty fathoms was the height of that cliff along which he lay when he drank of the water below. Then Sigurd spake --

"How sayedst thou, Regin, that this drake (1) was no greater than other ling-worms; methinks the track of him is marvellous great?"

Then said Regin, "Make thee a hole, and sit down therein, and whenas the worm comes to the water, smite him into the heart, and so do him to death, and win thee great fame thereby."

But Sigurd said, "What will betide me if I be before the blood of the worm?"

Says Regin, "Of what avail to counsel thee if thou art still afeard of everything? Little art thou like thy kin in stoutness of heart."

Then Sigurd rides right over the heath; but Regin gets him gone, sore afeard.

But Sigurd fell to digging him a pit, and whiles he was at that work, there came to him an old man with a long beard, and asked what he wrought there, and he told him.

Then answered the old man and said, "Thou doest after sorry counsel: rather dig thee many pits, and let the blood run therein; but sit thee down in one thereof, and so thrust the worm's heart through."

And therewithal he vanished away; but Sigurd made the pits even as it was shown to him.

Now crept the worm down to his place of watering, and the earth shook all about him, and he snorted forth venom on all the way before him as he went; but Sigurd neither trembled nor was adrad at the roaring of him. So whenas the worm crept over the pits, Sigurd thrust his sword under his left shoulder, so that it sank in up to the hilts; then up leapt Sigurd from the pit and drew the sword back again unto him, and therewith was his arm all bloody, up to the very shoulder.

Now when that mighty worm was ware that he had his death-wound, then he lashed out head and tail, so that all things soever that were before him were broken to pieces.

So whenas Fafnir had his death-wound, he asked "Who art thou? And who is thy father? And what thy kin, that thou wert so hardy as to bear weapons against me?"

Sigurd answered, "Unknown to men is my kin. I am called a noble beast: (2) neither father have I nor mother, and all alone have I fared hither."

Said Fafnir, "Whereas thou hast neither father nor mother, of what wonder weft thou born then? But now, though thou tellest me not thy name on this my death-day, yet thou knowest verily that thou liest unto me."

He answered, "Sigurd am I called, and my father was Sigmund."

Says Fafnir, "Who egged thee on to this deed, and why wouldst thou be driven to it? Hadst thou never heard how that all folk were adrad of me, and of the awe of my countenance? But an eager father thou hadst, O bright eyed swain!"

Sigurd answered, "A hardy heart urged me on hereto, and a strong hand and this sharp sword, which well thou knowest now, stood me in stead in the doing of the deed. `Seldom hath hardy eld a faint-heart youth.'"

Fafnir said, "Well, I wot that hadst thou waxed amid thy kin, thou mightest have good skill to slay folk in thine anger; but more of a marvel is it, that thou, a bondsman taken in war, shouldst have the heart to set on me, `for few among bondsmen have heart for the fight.'"

Said 8igurd, "Wilt thou then cast it in my teeth that I am far away from my kin? Albeit I was a bondsman, yet was I never shackled. God wot thou hast found me free enow."

Fafnir answered, "In angry wise dost thou take my speech; but hearken, for that same gold which I have owned shall be thy bane too."

Quoth Sigurd, "Fain would we keep all our wealth til that day of days; yet shall each man die once for all."

Said Fafnir, "Few things wilt thou do after my counsel, but take heed that thou shalt be drowned if thou farest unwarily over the sea; so bide thou rather on the dry land for the coming of the calm tide."

Then said Sigurd, "Speak, Fafnir, and say, if thou art so exceeding wise, who are the Norns who rule the lot of all mothers' sons."

Fafnir answers, "Many there be and wide apart; for some are of the kin of the Aesir, and some are of Elfin kin, and some there are who are daughters of Dvalin."

Said Sigurd, "How namest thou the holm whereon Surt (3) and the Aesir mix and mingle the water of the sword?"

"Unshapen is that holm hight," said Fafnir.

And yet again he said, "Regin, my brother, has brought about my end, and it gladdens my heart that thine too he bringeth about; for thus will things be according to his will."

And once again he spake, "A countenance of terror I bore up before all folk, after that I brooded over the heritage of my brother, and on every side did I spout out poison, so that none durst come anigh me, and of no weapon was I adrad, nor ever had I so many men before me, as that I deemed myself not stronger than all; for all men were sore afeard of me."

Sigurd answered and said, "Few may have victory by means of that same countenance of terror, for whoso comes amongst many shall one day find that no one man is by so far the mightiest of all."

Then says Fafnir, "Such counsel I give thee, that thou take thy horse and ride away at thy speediest, for ofttimes it fails out so, that he who gets a death-wound avenges himself none the less."

Sigurd answered, "Such as thy redes are I will nowise do after them; nay, I will ride now to thy lair and take to me that great treasure of thy kin."

"Ride there then," said Fafnir, "and thou shalt find gold enow to suffice thee for all thy life-days; yet shall that gold be thy bane, and the bane of every one soever who owns it."

Then up stood Sigurd, and said, "Home would I ride and lose all that wealth, if I deemed that by the losing thereof I should never die; but every brave and true man will fain have his hand on wealth till that last day that thou, Fafnir, wallow in the death-pain til Death and Hell have thee."

And therewithal Fafnir died.

ENDNOTES:

(1) Lat. "draco", a dragon.
(2) "Unknown to men is my kin." Sigurd refusing to tell his
    name is to be referred to the superstition that a dying man
    could throw a curse on his enemy.
(3) Surt; a fire-giant, who will destroy the world at the
    Ragnarok, or destruction of all things. Aesir; the gods.

CHAPTER XIX. Of the Slaying of Regin, Son of Hreidmar.

Thereafter came Regin to Sigurd, and said, "Hail, lord and master, a noble victory hast thou won in the slaying of Fafnir, whereas none durst heretofore abide in the path of him; and now shall this deed of fame be of renown while the world stands fast."

Then stood Regin staring on the earth a long while, and presently thereafter spake from heavy-mood: "Mine own brother hast thou slain, and scarce may I be called sackless of the deed."

Then Sigurd took his sword Gram and dried it on the earth, and spake to Regin
--

"Afar thou faredst when I wrought this deed and tried this sharp sword with the hand and the might of me; with all the might and main of a dragon must I strive, while thou wert laid alow in the heather-bush, wotting not if it were earth or heaven."

Said Regin, "Long might this worm have lain in his lair, if the sharp sword I forged with my hand had not been good at need to thee; had that not been, neither thou nor any man would have prevailed against him as at this time."

Sigurd answers, "Whenas men meet foes in fight, better is stout heart than sharp sword."

Then said Regin, exceeding heavily, "Thou hast slain my brother, and scarce may I be sackless of the deed."

Therewith Sigurd cut out the heart of the worm with the sword called Ridil; but Regin drank of Fafnir's blood, and spake, "Grant me a boon, and do a thing little for thee to do. Bear the heart to the fire, and roast it, and give me thereof to eat."

Then Sigurd went his ways and roasted it on a rod; and when the blood bubbled out he laid his finger thereon to essay it, if it were fully done; and then he set his finger in his mouth, and lo, when the heart-blood of the worm touched his tongue, straightway he knew the voice of all fowls, and heard withal how the wood- peckers chattered in the brake beside him --

"There sittest thou, Sigurd, roasting Fafnir's heart for another, that thou shouldest eat thine ownself, and then thou shouldest become the wisest of all men."

And another spake: "There lies Regin, minded to beguile the man who trusts in him."

But yet again said the third, "Let him smite the head from off him then, and be only lord of all that gold."

And once more the fourth spake and said, "Ah, the wiser were he if he followed after that good counsel, and rode thereafter to Fafnir's lair, and took to him that mighty treasure that lieth there, and then rode over Hindfell, whereas sleeps Brynhild; for there would he get great wisdom. Ah, wise he were, if he did after your redes, and bethought him of his own weal; `for where wolf's ears are, wolf's teeth are near.'"

Then cried the fifth: "Yea, yea, not so wise is he as I deem him, if he spareth him whose brother he hath slain already."

At last spake the sixth: "Handy and good rede to slay him, and be lord of the treasure!"

Then said Sigurd, "The time is unborn wherein Regin shall be my bane; nay, rather one road shall both these brothers fare."

And therewith he drew his sword Gram and struck off Regin's head.

Then heard Sigurd the wood-peckers a-singing, even as the song says. (1)

For the first sang:

"Bind thou, Sigurd,
The bright red rings!
Not meet it is
Many things to fear.
A fair may know I,
Fair of all the fairest
Girt about with gold,
Good for thy getting."

"Green go the ways
Toward the hall of Giuki
That the fates show forth
To those who fare thither;
There the rich king
Reareth a daughter;
Thou shalt deal, Sigurd,
With gold for thy sweetling."

And the third:

"A high hall is there
Reared upon Hindfell,
Without all around it
Sweeps the red flame aloft.
Wise men wrought
That wonder of halls
With the unhidden gleam
Of the glory of gold."

Then the fourth sang:

"Soft on the fell
A shield-may sleepeth
The lime-trees' red plague
Playing about her:
The sleep-thorn set Odin
Into that maiden
For her choosing in war
The one he willed not.

"Go, son, behold

That may under helm
Whom from battle
Vinskornir bore,
From her may not turn
The torment of sleep.
Dear offspring of kings
In the dread Norns' despite."

Then Sigurd ate some deal of Fafnir's heart, and the remnant he kept. Then he leapt on his horse and rode along the trail of the worm Fafnir, and so right unto his abiding-place; and he found it open, and beheld all the doors and the gear of them that they were wrought of iron: yea, and all the beams of the house; and it was dug down deep into the earth: there found Sigurd gold exceeding plenteous, and the sword Rotti; and thence he took the Helm of Awe, and the Gold Byrny, and many things fair and good. So much gold he found there, that he thought verily that scarce might two horses, or three belike, bear it thence. So he took all the gold and laid it in two great chests, and set them on the horse Grani, and took the reins of him, but nowise will he stir, neither will he abide smiting. Then Sigurd knows the mind of the horse, and leaps on the back of him, and smites and spurs into him, and off the horse goes even as if he were unladen.

ENDNOTES:

(1) The Songs of the Birds were inserted from "Reginsmal" by the translators.

CHAPTER XX. Of Sigurd's Meeting with Brynhild on the Mountain.

By long roads rides Sigurd, till he comes at the last up on to Hindfell, and wends his way south to the land of the Franks; and he sees before him on the fell a great light, as of fire burning, and flaming up even unto the heavens; and when he came thereto, lo, a shield hung castle before him, and a banner on the topmost thereof: into the castle went Sigurd, and saw one lying there asleep, and all-armed. Therewith he takes the helm from off the head of him, and sees that it is no man, but a woman; and she was clad in a byrny as closely set on her as though it had gown to her flesh; so he rent it from the collar downwards; and then the sleeves thereof, and ever the sword bit on it as if it were cloth. Then said Sigurd that over-long had she lain asleep; but she asked --

"What thing of great might is it that has prevailed to rend my byrny, and draw me from my sleep?"

Even as sings the song   (1)

> "What bit on the byrny,
> Why breaks my sleep away,
> Who has turned from me
> My wan tormenting?"

"Ah, is it so, that here is come Sigurd Sigmundson, bearing Fafnir's helm on his head and Fafnir's bane in his hand?"

Then answered Sigurd --

> "Sigmund's son

With Sigurd's sword
E'en now rent down
The raven's wall."

"Of the Volsung's kin is he who has done the deed; but now I have heard that thou art daughter of a mighty king, and folk have told us that thou wert lovely and full of lore, and now I will try the same."

Then Brynhild sang --

"Long have I slept
And slumbered long,
Many and long are the woes of mankind,
By the might of Odin
Must I bide helpless
To shake from off me the spells of slumber.
"Hail to the day come back!
Hail, sons of the daylight!
Hail to thee, dark night, and thy daughter!
Look with kind eyes a-down,
On us sitting here lonely,
And give unto us the gain that we long for.
"Hail to the Aesir,
And the sweet Asyniur! (2)
Hail to the fair earth fulfilled of plenty!
Fair words, wise hearts,
Would we win from you,
And healing hands while life we hold."

Then Brynhild speaks again and says, "Two kings fought, one hight Helm Gunnar, an old man, and the greatest of warriors, and Odin had promised the victory unto him; but his foe was Agnar, or Audi's brother, and so I smote down Helm Gunnar in the fight; and Odin, in vengeance for that deed, stuck the sleep-thorn into me, and said that I should never again have the victory, but should be given away in marriage; but there against I vowed a vow, that never would I wed one who knew the name of fear."

Then said Sigurd, "Teach us the lore of mighty matters!"

She said, "Belike thou cannest more skill in all than I; yet will I teach thee; yea, and with thanks, if there be aught of my cunning that will in anywise pleasure thee, either of runes or of other matters that are the root of things; but now let us drink together, and may the Gods give to us twain a good day, that thou mayst win good help and fame from my wisdom, and that thou mayst hereafter mind thee of that which we twain speak together."

Then Brynhild filled a beaker and bore it to Sigurd, and gave him the drink of love, and spake --

> "Beer bring I to thee,
> Fair fruit of the byrnies' clash,
> Mixed is it mightily,
> Mingled with fame,
> Brimming with bright lays
> And pitiful runes,
> Wise words, sweet words,
> Speech of great game.
>
> "Runes of war know thou,
> If great thou wilt be!
> Cut them on hilt of hardened sword,
> Some on the brand's back,
> Some on its shining side,
> Twice name Tyr therein.
>
> "Sea-runes good at need,
> Learnt for ship's saving,
> For the good health of the swimming horse;
> On the stern cut them,
> Cut them on the rudder-blade

And set flame to shaven oar:
  Howso big be the sea-hills,
  Howso blue beneath,
Hail from the main then comest thou home.

  "Word-runes learn well
  If thou wilt that no man
Pay back grief for the grief thou gavest;
  Wind thou these,
  Weave thou these,
Cast thou these all about thee,
  At the Thing,
  Where folk throng,
Unto the full doom faring.

  "Of ale-runes know the wisdom
  If thou wilt that another's wife
Should not bewray thine heart that trusteth:
  Cut them on the mead-horn,
  On the back of each hand,
And nick an N upon thy nail.

  "Ale have thou heed
  To sign from all harm
Leek lay thou in the liquor,
  Then I know for sure
  Never cometh to thee,
Mead with hurtful matters mingled.

  "Help-runes shalt thou gather
  If skill thou wouldst gain
To loosen child from low-laid mother;
  Cut be they in hands hollow,

Wrapped the joints round about;
Call for the Good-folks' gainsome helping.

"Learn the bough-runes wisdom
  If leech-lore thou lovest;
And wilt wot about wounds' searching
  On the bark be they scored;
  On the buds of trees
Whose boughs look eastward ever.

"Thought-runes shalt thou deal with
  If thou wilt be of all men
Fairest-souled wight, and wisest,
  These areded
  These first cut
These first took to heart high Hropt.

"On the shield were they scored
That stands before the shining God,
On Early-waking's ear,
On All-knowing's hoof,
On the wheel which runneth
Under Rognir's chariot;
On Sleipnir's jaw-teeth,
On the sleigh's traces.

"On the rough bear's paws,
And on Bragi's tongue,
On the wolfs claws,
And on eagle's bill,
On bloody wings,
And bridge's end;
On loosing palms,

And pity's path:

"On glass, and on gold,
And on goodly silver,
In wine and in wort,
And the seat of the witch-wife;
On Gungnir's point,
And Grani's bosom;
On the Norn's nail,
And the neb of the night-owl.

"All these so cut,
  Were shaven and sheared,
And mingled in with holy mead,
And sent upon wide ways enow;
  Some abide with the Elves,
  Some abide with the Aesir,
Or with the wise Vanir,
Some still hold the sons of mankind.

"These be the book-runes,
  And the runes of good help,
And all the ale-runes,
And the runes of much might;
  To whomso they may avail,
  Unbewildered unspoilt;
They are wholesome to have:
Thrive thou with these then.
When thou hast learnt their lore,
Till the Gods end thy life-days.

"Now shalt thou choose thee
  E'en as choice is bidden,

Sharp steel's root and stem,
  Choose song or silence;
  See to each in thy heart,
All hurt has been heeded."

Then answered Sigurd --

"Ne'er shall I flee,
Though thou wottest me fey;
Never was I born for blenching,
Thy loved rede will I
  Hold aright in my heart
Even as long as I may live."

ENDNOTES:

(1) The stanzas on the two following pages were inserted here
     from "Sigrdrifasmal" by the translators.
(2) Goddesses.

CHAPTER XXI. More Wise Words of Brynhild.

Sigurd spake now, "Sure no wiser woman than thou art one may be found in the wide world; yea, yea, teach me more yet of thy wisdom!"

She answers, "Seemly is it that I do according to thy will, and show thee forth more redes of great avail, for thy prayer's sake and thy wisdom ;" and she spake withal --

"Be kindly to friend and kin, and reward not their trespasses against thee; bear and forbear, and win for thee thereby long enduring praise of men.

"Take good heed of evil things: a may's love, and a man's wife; full oft thereof doth ill befall!

"Let not thy mind be overmuch crossed by unwise men at thronged meetings of folk; for oft these speak worse than they wot of; lest thou be called a dastard, and art minded to think that thou art even as is said; slay such an one on another day, and so reward his ugly talk.

"If thou farest by the way whereas bide evil things, be well ware of thyself; take not harbour near the highway, though thou be benighted, for oft abide there ill wights for men's bewilderment.

"Let not fair women beguile thee, such as thou mayst meet at the feast, so that the thought thereof stand thee in stead of sleep, and a quiet mind; yea, draw them not to thee with kisses or other sweet things of love.

"If thou hearest the fool's word of a drunken man, strive not with him being drunk with drink and witless; many a grief, yea, and the very death, groweth from out such things.

"Fight thy foes in the field, nor be burnt in thine house.

'Never swear thou wrongsome oath; great and grim is the reward for the breaking of plighted troth.

"Give kind heed to dead men, -- sick-dead, Sea-dead, or ˜word- dead; deal heedfully with their dead corpses.

"Trow never in him for whom thou hast slain father, brother, or whatso near kin, yea, though young he be; `for oft waxes wolf in youngling'.

"Look thou with good heed to the wiles of thy friends; but little skill is given to me, that I should foresee the ways of thy life; yet good it were that hate fell not on thee from those of thy wife's house."

Sigurd spake, "None among the sons of men can be found wiser than thou; and thereby swear I, that thee will I have as my own, for near to my heart thou liest."

She answers, "Thee would I fainest choose, though I had all men's sons to choose from."

And thereto they plighted troth both of them.

CHAPTER XXII. Of the Semblance and Array of Sigurd Fafnir's bane. (1)

Now Sigurd rides away; many-folded is his shield, an blazing with red gold, and the image of a dragon is drawn thereon; and this same was dark brown above, and bright red below; and with even such-like image was adorned helm, and saddle, and coat-armour; and he was clad in the golden byrny, and all his weapons were gold wrought.

Now for this cause was the drake drawn on all his weapons, that when he was seen of men, all folk might know who went there; yea, all those who had heard of his slaying of that great dragon, that the Voerings call Fafnir, and for that cause are his weapons gold-wrought, and brown of hue, and that he was by far above other men in courtesy and goodly manners, and well-nigh in all things else; and whenas folk tell of all the mightiest champions, and the noblest chiefs, then ever is he named the foremost, and his name goes wide about on all tongues north of the sea of the Greek-lands, and even so shall it be while the world endures.

Now the hair of this Sigurd was golden-red of hue, fair of fashion, and falling down in great locks; thick and short was his beard, and of no other colour, high-nosed he was, broad and high- boned of face; so keen were his eyes, that few durst gaze up under the brows of him; his shoulders were as broad to look on as the shoulders of two; most duly was his body fashioned betwixt height and breadth, and in such wise as was seemliest; and this is the sign told of his height, that when he was girt with his sword Gram, which same was seven spans long, as he went through the full-grown rye-fields, the dew-shoe of the said sword smote the ears of the standing corn; and, for all that, ;˜greater was his strength than his growth: well could he wield sword, and cast forth spear, shoot shaft, and hold shield, bend bow, back horse, and do all the goodly deeds that he learned in his youth's days.

Wise he was to know things yet undone; and the voice of all fowls he knew, wherefore few things fell on him unawares.

Of many words he was and so fair of speech withal, that whensoever he made it his business to speak, he never left speaking before that to all men it seemed full sure, that no otherwise must the matter be than as he said.

His sport and pleasure it was to give aid to his own folk, and to prove himself in mighty matters, to take wealth from his unfriends, and give the same to his friends.

Never did he lose heart, and of naught was he adrad.

ENDNOTES:

(1) This chapter is nearly literally the same as chapter 166 of the "Wilkinasaga"; Ed.: Perinskiold, Stockholm, 1715.

CHAPTER XXIII. Sigurd comes to Hlymdale.

Forth Sigurd fides till he comes to a great and goodly dwelling, the lord whereof was a mighty chief called Heimir; he had to wife a sister of Brynhild, who was hight Bekkhild, because she had bidden at home, and learned handicraft, whereas Brynhild fared with helm and byrny, unto the wars, wherefore was she called Brynhild.

Heimir and Bekkhild had a son called Alswid, the most courteous of men.

Now at this stead were men disporting them abroad, but when they see the man riding thereto, they leave their play to wonder at him, for none such had they ever seen erst, so they went to meet him, and gave him good welcome. Alswid bade him abide and have such things at his hands as he would; and he takes his bidding blithesomely; due service withal was established for him; four men bore the treasure of gold from off the horse, and the fifth took it to him to guard the same; therein were many things to behold, things of great price, and seldom seen; and great game and joy men had to look on byrnies and helms, and mighty rings, and wondrous great golden stoups, and all kinds of war weapons.

So there dwelt Sigurd long in great honour holden; and tidings of that deed of fame spread wide through all lands, of how he had slain that hideous and fearful dragon. So good joyance had they there together, and each was leal to other; and their sport was in the arraying of their weapons, and the shafting of their arrows, and the flying of their falcons.

CHAPTER XXIV. Sigurd sees Brynhild at Hlymdale.

In those days came home to Heimir, Brynhild, his foster daughter, and she sat in her bower with her maidens, and could do more skill in handycraft than other women; she sat, overlaying cloth with gold, and sewing therein the great deeds which Sigurd had wrought, the slaying of the Worm, and the taking of the wealth of him, and the death of Regin withal.

Now tells the tale, that on a day Sigurd rode into the wood with hawk, and hound, and men thronging; and whenas he came home his hawk flew up to a high tower and sat him down on a certain window. Then fared Sigurd after his hawk, and he saw where sat a fair woman, and knew that it was Brynhild, and he deems all things he sees there to be worthy together, both her fairness, and the fair things she wrought: and therewith he goes into the hall, but has no more joyance in the games of the men folk.

Then spake Alswid, "Why art thou so bare of bliss; this manner of thine grieveth us thy friends; why then wilt thou not hold to thy gleesome ways? Lo, thy hawks pine now, and thy horse Grani droops; and long will it be ere we are booted thereof?"

Sigurd answered, "Good friend, hearken to what lies on my mind; for my hawk flew up into a certain tower; and when I came thereto and took him, lo there I saw a fair woman, and she sat by a needlework of gold, and did thereon, my deeds that are passed, and my deeds that are to come,"

Then said Alswid, "Thou has seen Brynhild, Budli's daughter, the greatest of great women."

"Yea, verily," said Sigurd; "but how came she hither?"

Aswid answered, "Short space there was betwixt the coming hither of the twain of you."

Says Sigurd, "Yea, but a few, days agone I knew her for the best of the world's women."

Alswid said, "Give not all thine heed to one woman, being such a man as thou art; ill life to sit lamenting for what we may not have."

"I shall go meet her," says Sigurd, "and get from her love like my love, and give her a gold ring in token thereof."

Alswid answered, "None has ever yet been known whom she would let sit beside her, or to whom she would give drink; for ever will she hold to warfare and to the winning of all kinds of fame."

Sigurd said, "We know not for sure whether she will give us answer or not, or grant us a seat beside her."

So the next day after, Sigurd went to the bower, but Alswid stood outside the bower door, fitting shafts to his arrows.

Now Sigurd spake, "Abide, fair and hale lady, -- how farest thou?"

She answered, "Well it fares; my kin and my friends live yet: but who shall say what goodhap folk may bear to their life's end?"

He sat him down by her, and there came in four damsels with great golden beakers, and the best of wine therein; and these stood before the twain.

Then said Brynhild, "This seat is for few, but and if my father come."

He answered, "Yet is it granted to one that likes me well."

Now that chamber was hung with the best and fairest of hanging, and the floor thereof was all covered with cloth.

Sigurd spake, "Now has it come to pass even as thou didst promise."

"O be thou welcome here!" said she, and arose there with, and the four damsels with her, and bore the golden beaker to him, and bade him drink; he stretched oui his hand to the beaker, and took it, and her hand withal, and drew her down beside him; and cast his arms round about her neck and kissed her, and said --

"Thou art the fairest that was ever born!"

But Brynhild said, "Ah, wiser is it not to cast faith and troth into a woman's power, for ever shall they break that they have promised."

He said, "That day would dawn the best of days over our heads whereon each of each should be made happy."

Brynhild answered, "It is not fated that we should abide together; I am a shield-may, and wear helm on head even as the kings of war, and them full oft I help, neither is the battle become loathsome to me."

Sigurd answered, "What fruit shall be of our life, if we live not together: harder to bear this pain that lies hereunder, than the stroke of sharp sword."

Brynhild answers, "I shall gaze on the hosts of the war kings, but thou shalt wed Gudrun, the daughter of Giuki."

Sigurd answered, "What king's daughter lives to beguile me? Neither am I double-hearted herein; and now I swear by the Gods that thee shall I have for mine own, or no woman else.

And even suchlike wise spake she.

8igurd thanked her for her speech, and gave her a gold ring, and now they swore oath anew, and so he went his ways to his men, and is with them awhile in great bliss.

CHAPTER XXV. Of the Dream of Gudrun, Giuki's daughter.

There was a king hight Giuki, who ruled a realm south of the Rhine; three sons he had, thus named: Gunnar, Hogni, and Guttorm, and Gudrun was the name of his daughter, the fairest of maidens; and all these children were far before all other king's children in all prowess, and in goodliness and growth withal; ever were his sons at the wars and wrought many a deed of fame. But Giuki had wedded Grimhild the Wise-wife.

Now Budli was the name of a king mightier than Giuki, mighty though they both were: and Atli was the brother of Brynhild: Atli was a fierce man and a grim, great and black to look on, yet noble of mien withal, and the greatest of warriors. Grimhild was a fierce-heart woman.

Now the days of the Giukings bloomed fair, and chiefly because of those children, so far before the sons of men.

On a day Gudrun says to her mays that she may have no joy of heart; then a certain woman asked her wherefore her joy was departed.

She answered, "Grief came to me in my dreams, therefore is there sorrow in my heart, since thou must needs ask thereof."

"Tell it me, then, thy dream," said the woman, "for dreams oft forecast but the weather."

Gudrun answers, "Nay, nay, no weather is this; I dreamed that I had a fair hawk on my wrist, feathered with feathers of gold."

Says the woman, "Many have heard tell of thy beauty, thy wisdom, and thy courtesy; some king's son abides thee, then."

Gudrun answers, "I dreamed that naught was so dear to me as this hawk, and all my wealth had I cast aside rather than him."

The woman said, "Well, then, the man thou shalt have will be of the goodliest, and well shalt thou love him."

Gudrun answered, "It grieves me that I know not who he shall be; let us go seek Brynhild, for she belike will wot thereof."

So they arrayed them in gold and many a fair thing, and she went with her damsels till they came to the hall of Brynhild, and that hall was dight with gold, and stood on a high hill; and whenas their goings were seen, it was told Brynhild, that a company of women drove toward the burg in gilded waggons.

"That shall be Gudrun, Giuki's daughter," says she: "I dreamed of her last night; let us go meet her! No fairer woman may come to our house."

So they went abroad to meet them, and gave them good greeting, and they went into the goodly hall together; fairly painted it was within, and well adorned with silver vessel; cloths were spread under the feet of them, and all folk served them, and in many wise they sported.

But Gudrun was somewhat silent.

Then said Brynhild, "Ill to abash folk of their mirth; prithee do not so; let us talk together for our disport of mighty kings and their great deeds."

"Good talk," says Gudrun, "let us do even so; what kings deemest thou to have been the first of all men?"

Brynhild says, "The sons of Haki, and Hagbard withal; they brought to pass many a deed of fame in the warfare."

Gudrun answers, "Great men certes, and of noble fame! Yet Sigar took their one sister, and burned the other, house and all; and they may be called slow to revenge the deed; why didst thou not name my brethren who are held to be the first of men as at this time?"

Brynhild says, "Men of good hope are they surely though but little proven hitherto; but one I know far before them, Sigurd, the son of Sigmund the king; a youngling was he in the days when he slew the sons of Hunding, and revenged his father, and Eylimi, his mother's father."

Said Gudrun, "By what token tellest thou that?"

Brynhild answered, "His mother went amid the dead and found Sigmund the king sore wounded, and would bind up his hurts; but he said he grew over old for war; and bade her lay this comfort to her heart, that she should bear the most famed of sons; and wise was the wise man's word therein: for after the death of King Sigmund, she went to King Alf, and there was Sigurd nourished in great honour, and day by day he wrought some deed of fame, and is the man most renowned of all the wide world."

Gudrun says, "From love hast thou gained these tidings of him; but for this cause came I here, to tell thee dreams of mine which have brought me great grief."

Says Brynhild, "Let not such matters sadden thee: abide with thy friends who wish thee blithesome, all of them!"

"This I dreamed," said Gudrun, "that we went, a many of us in company, from the bower, and we saw an exceeding great hart, that far excelled all other deer ever seen, and the hair of him was golden; and this deer we were all fain to take, but I alone got him; and he seemed to me better than all things else; but sithence thou, Byrnhild, didst shoot and slay my deer even at my very knees, and such grief was that to me that scarce might I bear it; and then afterwards thou gavest me a wolf-cub, which besprinkled me with the blood of my brethren."

Brynhild answers, "I will arede thy dream, even as things shall come to pass hereafter; for Sigurd shall come to thee, even he whom I have chosen for my well-beloved; and Grimhild shall give him mead mingled with hurtful things, which shall cast us all into mighty strife. Him shalt thou have, and him shalt thou quickly miss; and Atli the king shalt thou wed; and thy brethren shalt thou lose, and slay Atli withal in the end."

Dudrun answers, "Grief and woe to know that such things shall be!"

And therewith she and hers get them gone home to King Giuki.

CHAPTER XXVI.

Now Sigurd goes his ways with all that great treasure, and in friendly wise he departs from them; and on Grani he rides with all his war-gear and the burden withal; and thus he rides until he comes to the hall of King Giuki; there he rides into the burg, and that sees one of the king's men, and he spake withal --

"Sure it may be deemed that here is come one of the Gods, for his array is all done with gold, and his horse is far mightier than other horses, and the manner of his weapons is most exceeding goodly, and most of all the man himself far excels all other men ever seen."

So the king goes out with his court and greets the man, and asks --

"Who art thou who thus ridest into my burg, as none has durst hitherto without the leave of my sons?"

He answered, "I am called Sigurd, son of King Sigmund."

Then said King Giuki, "Be thou welcome here then, and take at our hands whatso thou wiliest."

So he went into the king's hall, and all men seemed little beside him, and all men served him, and there he abode in great joyance.

Now oft they all ride abroad together, Sigurd and Gunnar and Hogni, and ever is Sigurd far the foremost of them, mighty men of their hands though they were.

But Grimhild finds how heartily Sigurd loved Brynhild, and how oft he talks of her; and she falls to thinking how well it were, if he might abide there and wed the daughter of King Giuki, for she saw that none might come anigh to his goodliness, and what faith and goodhelp there was in him, and how that he had more wealth withal than folk might tell of any man; and the king did to him even as unto his own sons, and they for their parts held him of more worth than themselves.

So on a night as they sat at the drink, the queen arose, and went before Sigurd, and said --

"Great joy we have in thine abiding here, and all good things will we put before thee to take of us; lo now, take this horn and drink thereof."

So he took it and drank, and therewithal she said, "Thy father shall be Giuki the king, and I shall be thy mother, and Gunnar and Hogni shall be thy brethren, and all this shall be sworn with oaths each to each; and then surely shall the like of you never be found on earth."

Sigurd took her speech well, for with the drinking of that drink all memory of Brynhild departed from him. So there he abode awhile.

And on a day went Grimhild to Giuki the king, and cast her arms about his neck, and spake --

"Behold, there has now come to us the greatest of great hearts that the world holds; and needs must he be trusty and of great avail; give him thy daughter then, with plenteous wealth, and as much of rule as he will; perchance thereby he will be well content to abide here ever."

The king answered, "Seldom does it befall that kings offer their daughters to any; yet in higher wise will it be done to offer her to this man, than to take lowly prayers to her from others."

On a night Gudrun pours out the drink, and Sigurd beholds her how fair she is and how full of all courtesy.

Five seasons Sigurd abode there, and ever they passed their days together in good honour and friendship.

And so it befell that the king held talk together, and Giuki said --

"Great good thou givest us, Sigurd, and with exceeding strength thou strengthenest our realm."

Then Gunnar said, "All things that may be will we do for thee, so thou abidest here long; both dominion shalt thou have, and our sister freely and unprayed for, whom another man would not get for all his prayers."

Sigurd says, "Thanks have ye for this wherewith; ye honour me, and gladly will I take the same."

Therewith they swore brotherhood together, and to be even as if they were children of one father and one mother; and a noble feast was holden, and endured many days, and Sigurd drank at the wedding of him and Gudrun; and there might men behold all manner of game and glee, and each day the feast was better and better.

Now fare these folk wide over the world, and do many great deeds, and slay many kings' sons, and no man has ever done such works of prowess as did they; then home they come again with much wealth won in war.

Sigurd gave of the serpent's heart to Gudrun, and she ate thereof, and became greater-hearted, and wiser than ere before: and the son of these twain was called Sigmund.

Now on a time went Grimhild to Gunnar her son, and spake --

"Fair blooms the life and fortune of thee, but for one thing only, and namely whereas thou art unwedded; go woo Brynhild; good rede is this, and Sigurd will ride with thee."

Gunnar answered, "Fair in she certes, and I am fain enow to win her;" and therewith he tells his father, and his brethren, and Sigurd, and they all prick him on to that wooing.

CHAPTER XXVII. The Wooing of Brynhild.

Now they array them joyously for their journey, and ride over hill and dale to the house of King Budli, and woo his daughter of him; in a good wise he took their speech, if so be that she herself would not deny them, but he said withal that so high- minded was she, that that man only might wed her whom she would.

Then they ride to Hlymdale, and there Heimir gave them good welcome; so Gunnar tells his errand; Heimir says, that she must needs wed but him whom she herself chose freely; and tells them how her abode was but a little way thence, and that he deemed that him only would she have who should ride through the flaming fire that was drawn round about her hall; so they depart and come to the hall and the fire, and see there a castle with a golden roof-ridge, and all round about a fire roaring up.

Now Gunnar rode on Goti, but Hogni on Holkvi, and Gunnar smote his horse to face the fire, but he shrank aback.

Then said Sigurd, "Why givest thou back, Gunnar?"

He answered, "The horse will not tread this fire; but lend me thy horse Grani."

"Yea, with all my good will," says Sigurd.

Then Gunnar rides him at the fire, and yet nowise will Gram stir, nor may Gunnar any the more ride through that fire. So now they change semblance, Gunnar and Sigurd, even as Grimhild had taught them; then Sigurd in the likeness of Gunnar mounts and rides, Gram in his hand, and golden spurs on his heels; then leapt Grani into the fire when he felt the spurs; and a mighty roar arose as the fire burned ever madder, and the earth trembled, and the flames went up even unto the heavens, nor had any dared to ride as he rode, even as it were through the deep mirk.

But now the fire sank withal, and he leapt from his horse and went into the hall, even as the song says --

> "The flame flared at its maddest,
> Earth's fields fell a-quaking
> As the red flame aloft
> Licked the lowest of heaven.
> Few had been fain,
> Of the rulers of folk,
> To ride through that flame,
> Or athwart it to tread.

> "Then Sigurd smote
> Grani with sword,
> And the flame was slaked
> Before the king;
> Low lay the flames
> Before the fain of fame;
> Bright gleamed the array
> That Regin erst owned.

Now when Sigurd had passed through the fire, he came into a certain fair dwelling, and therein sat Brynhild.

She asked, "What man is it?"

Then he named himself Gunnar, son of Giuki, and said -- "Thou art awarded to me as my wife, by the good will and word of thy father and thy foster-father, and I have ridden through the flame of thy fire, according to thy that thou hast set forth."

"I wot not clearly," said she, "how I shall answer thee."

Now Sigurd stood upright on the hall floor, and leaning on the hilt of his sword, and he spake to Brynhild --

"In reward thereof, shall I pay thee a great dower in gold and goodly things?"

She answered in heavy mood from her seat, whereas she sat like unto swan on billow, having a sword in her hand and a helm on her head, and being clad in a byrny, "O Gunnar," she says, "speak not to me of such things unless thou be the first and best of all men; for then shall thou slay those my wooers, if thou hast heart thereto; I have been in battles with the king of the Greeks, and weapons were stained with red blood, and for such things still I yearn."

He answered, "Yea, certes many great deeds hast thou done; but yet call thou to mind thine oath, concerning the riding through of this fire, wherein thou didst swear that thou wouldst go with the man who should do this deed."

So she found that he spoke but the sooth, and she paid heed to his words, and arose, and greeted him meetly, and he abode there three nights, and they lay in one bed together; but he took the sword Gram and laid it betwixt them: then she asked him why he laid it there; and he answered, that in that wise must he needs wed his wife or else get his bane.

Then she took from off her the ring Andvari's loom, which he had given her aforetime, and gave it to him, but he gave her another ring out of Fafnir's hoard.

Thereafter he rode away through the same fire unto his Fellows, and he and Gunnar changed semblances again, and rode unto Hlymdale, and told how it had gone with them.

That same day went Brynhild home to her foster-father, and tells him as one whom she trusted, how that there had come a king to her; "And he rode through my flaming fire, and said he was come to woo me, and named himself Gunnar; but I said that such a deed might Sigurd alone have done, with whom I plighted troth on the mountain; and he is my first troth-plight, and my well-beloved."

Heimir said that things must needs abide even as now they had now come to pass.

Brynhild said, "Aslaug the daughter of me and Sigurd shall be nourished here with thee."

Now the kings fare home, but Brynhild goes to her father; Grimhild welcomes the kings meetly, and thanks Sigurd for his fellowship; and withal is a great feast made, and many were the guests thereat; and thither came Budli the King with his daughter Brynhild, and his son Atli, and for many days did the feast endure: and at that feast was Gunnar wedded to Brynhild: but when it was brought to an end, once more has Sigurd memory of all the oaths that he sware unto Brynhild, yet withal he let all things abide in rest and peace.

Brynhild and Gunnar sat together in great game and glee, and drank goodly wine.

CHAPTER XXVIII. How the Queens held angry converse together at the Bathing.

On a day as the Queens went to the river to bathe them, Brynhild waded the farthest out into the river; then asked Gudrun what that deed might signify. Brynhild said, "Yea, and why then should I be equal to thee in this matter more than in others? I am minded to think that my father is mightier than thine, and my true love has wrought many wondrous works of fame, and hath ridden the flaming fire withal, while thy husband was but the thrall of King Hjalprek."

Gudrun answered full of wrath, "Thou wouldst be wise if thou shouldst hold thy peace rather than revile my husband: lo now, the talk of all men it is, that none has ever abode in this world like unto him in all matters soever; and little it beseems thee of all folk to mock him who was thy first beloved: and Fafnir he slew, yea, and he rode thy flaming fire, whereas thou didst deem that he was Gunnar the King, and by thy side he lay, and took from thine hand the ring Andvari's-loom; -- here mayst thou well behold it!"

Then Brynhild saw the ring and knew it, and waxed as wan as a dead woman, and she went home and spake no word the evening long.

So when Sigurd came to bed to Gudrun she asked him why Brynhild's joy was so departed.

He answered, "I know not, but sore I misdoubt me that soon we shall know thereof overwell."

Gudrun said, "Why may she not love her life, having wealth and bliss, and the praise of all men, and the man withal that she would have?"

"Ah, yea!" said Sigurd, "and where in all the world was she then, when she said that she deemed she had the noblest of all men, and the dearest to her heart of all?"

Gudrun answers, "Tomorn will I ask her concerning this, who is the liefest to her of all men for a husband."

Sigurd said, "Needs must I forbid thee this, and full surely wilt thou rue the deed if thou doest it."

Now the next morning they sat in the bower, and Brynhild was silent; then spake Gudrun --

"Be merry, Brynhild! Grievest thou because of that speech of ours together, or what other thing slayeth thy bliss?"

Brynhild answers, "With naught but evil intent thou sayest this, for a cruel heart thou hast."

"Say not so," said Gudrun; "but rather tell me all the tale."

Brynhild answers, "Ask such things only as are good for thee to know -- matters meet for mighty dames. Good to love good things when all goes according to thy heart's desire!"

Gudrun says, "Early days for me to glory in that; but this word of thine looketh toward some foreseeing. What ill dost thou thrust at us? I did naught to grieve thee."

Brynhild answers, "For this shalt thou pay, in that thou hast got Sigurd to thee, -- nowise can I see thee living in the bliss thereof, whereas thou hast him, and the wealth and the might of him."

But Gudrun answered, "Naught knew I of your words and vows together; and well might my father look to the mating of me without dealing with thee first."

"No secret speech had we," quoth Brynhild, "though we swore oath together; and full well didst thou know that thou wentest about to beguile me; verily thou shalt have thy reward!"

Says Gudrun, "Thou art mated better than thou are worthy of; but thy pride and rage shall be hard to slake belike, and there for shall many a man pay."

"Ah, I should be well content," said Brynhild, "if thou hadst not the nobler man!"

Gudrun answers, "So noble a husband hast thou, that who knows of a greater king or a lord of more wealth and might?"

Says Brynhild, "Sigurd slew Fafnir, and that only deed is of more worth than all the might of King Gunnar."

(Even as the song says) --

> "The worm Sigurd slew,
> Nor ere shall that deed
> Be worsened by age
> While the world is alive.
> But thy brother the King
> Never durst, never bore
> The flame to ride down
> Through the fire to fare."

Gudrun answers, "Grani would not abide the fire under Gunnar the King, but Sigurd durst the deed, and thy heart may well abide without mocking him."

Brynhild answers, "Nowise will I hide from thee that I deem no good of Grimhild."

Says Gudrun, "Nay, lay no ill words on her, for in all things she is to thee as to her own daughter."

"Ah," says Brynhild, "she is the beginning of all this hale that biteth so; an evil drink she bare to Sigurd, so that he had no more memory of my very name."

"All wrong thou talkest; a lie without measure is this," quoth Gudrun.

Brynhild answered, "Have thou joy of Sigurd according to the measure of the wiles wherewith ye have beguiled me! Unworthily have ye conspired against me; may all things go with you as my heart hopes!"

Gudrun says, "More joy shall I have of him than thy wish would give unto me: but to no man's mind it came, that he had aforetime his pleasure of me; nay not once."

"Evil speech thou speakest," says Brynhild; "when thy wrath runs off thou wilt rue it; but come now, let us no more cast angry words one at the other!"

Says Gudrun, "Thou wert the first to cast such words at me, and now thou makest as if thou wouldst amend it, but a cruel and hard heart abides behind."

"Let us lay aside vain babble," says Brynhild. "Long did I hold my peace concerning my sorrow of heart, and, lo now, thy brother alone do I love; let us fall to other talk."

Gudrun said, "Far beyond all this doth thine heart look."

And so ugly ill befell from that going to the river, and that knowing of the ring, wherefrom did all their talk arise.

CHAPTER XXIX. Of Brynhild's great Grief and Mourning.

After this talk Brynhild lay a-bed, and tidings were brought to King Gunnar that Brynhild was sick; he goes to see her thereon, and asks what ails her; but she answered him naught, but lay there as one dead: and when he was hard on her for an answer, she said --

"What didst thou with that ring that I gave thee, even the one which King Budli gave me at our last parting, when thou and King Giuki came to him and threatened fire and the sword, unless ye had me to wife? Yea, at that time he led me apart, and asked me which I had chosen of those who were come; but I prayed him that I might abide to ward the land and be chief over the third part of his men; then were there two choices for me to deal betwixt either that I should be wedded to him whom he would, or lose all my weal and friendship at his hands; and he said withal that his friendship would be better to me than his wrath: then I bethought me whether I should yield to his will, or slay many a man; and therewithal I deemed that it would avail little to strive with him, and so it fell out, that I promised to wed whomsoever should ride the horse Grani with Fafnir's Hoard, and ride through my flaming fire, and slay those men whom I called on him to slay, and now so it was, that none durst ride, save Sigurd only, because he lacked no heart thereto; yea, and the Worm he flew, and Regin, and five kings beside; but thou, Gunnar, durst do naught; as pale as a dead man didst thou wax, and no king thou art, and no champion; so whereas I made a vow unto my father, that him alone would I love who was the noblest man alive, and that this is none save Sigurd, lo, now have I broken my oath and brought it to naught, since he is none of mine, and for this cause shall I compass thy death; and a great reward of evil things have I wherewith to reward Grimhild; -- never, I wot, has woman lived eviler or of lesser heart than she."

Gunnar answered in such wise that few might hear him, "Many a vile word hast thou spoken, and an evil-hearted woman art thou, whereas thou revilest a woman far better than thou; never would she curse her life as thou dost; nay, nor has she tormented dead folk, or murdered any; but lives her life well praised of all."

Brynhild answered, "Never have I dwelt with evil things privily, or done loathsome deeds; -- yet most fain I am to slay thee."

And therewith would she slay King Gunnar, but Hogni laid her in fetters; but then Gunnar spake withal --

"Nay, I will not that she abide in fetters."

Then said she, "Heed it not! For never again seest thou me glad in thine hall, never drinking, never at the chess-play, never speaking the words of kindness, never over-laying the fair cloths with gold, never giving thee good counsel; -- ah, my sorrow of heart that I might not get Sigurd to me!"

Then she sat up and smote her needlework, and rent it asunder, and bade set open her bower doors, that far away might the wailings of her sorrow be heard; then great mourning and lamentation there was, so that folk heard far and wide through that abode.

Now Gudrun asked her bower-maidens why they sat so joyless and downcast. "What has come to you, that ye fare ye as witless women, or what unheard-of wonders have befallen you?"

Then answered a waiting lady, hight Swaflod, "An untimely, an evil day it is, and our hall is fulfilled of lamentation."

Then spake Gudrun to one of her handmaids, "Arise, for we have slept long; go, wake Brynhild, and let us fall to our needlework and be merry."

"Nay, nay," she says, "nowise may I wake her, or talk with her; for many days has she drunk neither mead nor wine; surely the wrath of the Gods has fallen upon her."

Then spake Gudrun to Gunnar, "Go and see her," she says, "and bid her know that I am grieved with her grief."

"Nay," says Gunnar, "I am forbid to go see her or to share her weal."

Nevertheless he went unto her, and strives in many wise to have speech of her, but gets no answer whatsoever; therefore he gets him gone and finds Hogni, and bids him go see her: he said he was loth thereto, but went, and gat no more of her.

Then they go and find Sigurd, and pray him to visit her; he answered naught thereto, and so matters abode for that night.

But the next day, when he came home from hunting, Sigurd went to Gudrun, and spake --

"In such wise do matters show to me, as though great and evil things will betide from this trouble and upheaving; and that Brynhild will surely die."

Gudrun answers, "O my lord, by great wonders is she encompassed, seven days and seven nights has she slept, and none has dared wake her."

"Nay, she sleeps not," said Sigurd, "her heart is dealing rather with dreadful intent against me."

Then said Gudrun, weeping, "Woe worth the while for thy death! Go and see her; and wot if her fury may not be abated; give her gold, and smother up her grief and anger therewith!"

Then Sigurd went out, and found the door of Brynhild's chamber open; he deemed she slept, and drew the clothes from off her, and said --

"Awake, Brynhild! The sun shineth now over all the house, and thou hast slept enough; cast off grief from thee, and take up gladness!"

She said, "And how then hast thou dared to come to me? In this treason none was worse to me than thou."

Said Sigurd, "Why wilt thou not speak to folk? For what cause sorrowest thou?"

Brynhild answers, "Ah, to thee will I tell of my wrath!"

Sigurd said, "As one under a spell art thou, if thou deemest that there is aught cruel in my heart against thee; but thou hast him for husband whom thou didst choose."

"Ah, nay," she said, "never did Gunnar ride through the fire to me, nor did he give me to dower the host of the slain: I wondered at the man who came into my hall; for I deemed indeed that I knew thine eyes; but I might not see clearly, or divide the good from the evil, because of the veil that lay heavy on my fortune."

Says Sigurd, "No nobler men are there than the sons of Giuki, they slew the king of the Danes, and that great chief, the brother of King Budli."

Brynhild answered, "Surely for many an ill-deed must I reward them; mind me not of my griefs against them! But thou, Sigurd, slewest the Worm, and rodest the fire through; yea, and for my sake, and not one of the sons of King Giuki."

Sigurd answers, "I am not thy husband, and thou art not my wife; yet did a farfamed king pay dower to thee."

Says Brynhild, "Never looked I at Gunnar in such a wise that my heart smiled on him; and hard and fell am I to him, though I hide it from others."

"A marvellous thing," says Sigurd, "not to love such a king; what angers thee most? For surely his love should be better to thee than gold."

"This is the sorest sorrow to me," she said, "that the bitter sword is not reddened in thy blood."

"Have no fear thereof!" says he, "no long while to wait or the bitter sword stand deep in my heart; and no worse needest thou to pray for thyself, for thou wilt not live when I am dead; the days of our two lives shall be few enough from henceforth."

Brynhild answers, "Enough and to spare of bale is in thy speech, since thou bewrayedst me, and didst twin (1) me and all bliss; -- naught do I heed my life or death."

Sigurd answers, "Ah, live, and love King Gunnar and me withal! And all my wealth will I give thee if thou die not."

Brynhild answers, "Thou knowest me not, nor the heart that is in me; for thou art the first and best of all men, and I am become the most loathsome of all woman to thee."

"This is truer," says Sigurd, "that I loved thee better than myself, though I fell into the wiles from whence our lives may not escape; for whenso my own heart and mind availed me, then I sorrowed sore that thou wert not my wife; but as I might I put my trouble from me, for in a king's dwelling was I; and withal and in spite of all I was well content that we were all together. Well may it be, that that shall come to pass which is foretold; neither shall I fear the fulfilment thereof."

Brynhild answered, and said, "Too late thou tellest me that my grief grieved thee: little pity shall I find now."

Sigurd said, "This my heart would, that thou and I should go into one bed together; even so wouldst thou be my wife."

Said Brynhild, "Such words may nowise be spoken, nor will I have two kings in one hall; I will lay my life down rather than beguile Gunnar the King."

And therewith she call to mind how they met, they two, on the mountain, and swore oath each to each.

"But now is all changed and I will not live."

"I might not call to mind thy name," said Sigurd, "or know time again, before the time of thy wedding; the greatest of all griefs is that."

Then said Brynhild, "I swore an oath to wed the man who should ride my flaming fire, and that oath will I hold to, or die."

"Rather than thou die, I will wed thee, and put away Gudrun." said Sigurd.

But therewithal so swelled the heart betwixt the sides of him, that the rings of his byrny burst asunder.

"I will not have thee," says Brynhild, "nay, nor any other!"

Then Sigurd got him gone.

So saith the song of Sigurd --

>"Out then went Sigurd,
>   The great kings' well-loved,
>   From the speech and the sorrow,
>   Sore drooping, so grieving,
>   That the shirt round about him
>   Of iron tings woven,
>   From the sides brake asunder
>   Of the brave in the battle."

So when Sigurd came into the hall, Gunnar asked if he had come to a knowledge of what great grief lay heavy on her, or if she had power of speech: and Sigurd said that she lacked it not. So now Gunnar goes to her again, and asked her, what wrought her woe, or if there were anything that might amend it.

"I will not live," says Brynhild, "for Sigurd has bewrayed me, yea, and thee no less, whereas thou didst suffer him to come into my bed: lo thou, two men in one dwelling I will not have; and this shall be Sigurd's death, or thy death, or my death; -- for now has he told Gudrun all, and she is mocking me even now!"

ENDNOTES: (1) Sunder.

CHAPTER XXX. Of the Slaying of Sigurd Fafnir's-bane.

Thereafter Brynhild went out, and sat under her bower-wall, and had many words of wailing to say, and still she cried that all things were loathsome to her, both land and lordship alike, so she might not have Sigurd. But therewith came Gunnar to her yet again, and Brynhild spake, "Thou shalt lose both realm and wealth, and thy life and me, for I shall fare home to my kin, and abide there in sorrow, unless thou slayest Sigurd and his son; never nourish thou a wolfcub."

Gunnar grew sick at heart thereat, and might nowise see what fearful thing lay beneath it all; he was bound to Sigurd by oath, and this way and that way swung the heart within him; but at the last he bethought him of the measureless shame if his wife went from him, and he said within himself, "Brynhild is better to me than all things else, and the fairest woman of all women, and I will lay down my life rather than lose the love of her." And herewith he called to him his brother and spake, --

"Trouble is heavy on me," and he tells him that he must needs slay Sigurd, for that he has failed him where in he trusted him; "so let us be lords of the gold and the realm withal."

Hogni answers, "Ill it behoves us to break our oaths with wrack and wrong, and withal great aid we have in him; no kings shall be as great as we, if so be the King of the Hun-folk may live; such another brother-in-law never may we get again; bethink thee how good it is to have such a brother-in-law, and such sons to our sister! But well I see how things stand, for this has Brynhild stirred thee up to, and surely shall her counsel drag us into huge shame and scathe."

Gunnar says, "Yet shall it be brought about: and, lo, a rede thereto; -- let us egg on our brother Guttorm to the deed; he is young, and of little knowledge, and is clean out of all the oaths moreover."

"Ah, set about in ill wise," says Hogni, "and though indeed it may well be compassed, a due reward shall we gain for the bewrayal of such a man as is Sigurd."

Gunnar says, "Sigurd shall die, or I shall die."

And therewith he bids Brynhild arise and be glad at heart: so she arose, and still ever she said that Gunnar should come no more into her bed till the deed was done.

So the brothers fall to talk, and Gunnar says that it is a deed well worthy of death, that taking of Brynhild's maidenhead; "So come now, let us prick on Guttorm to do the deed."

Therewith they call him to them, and offer him gold and great dominion, as they well have might to do. Yea, and they took a certain worm and somewhat of wolf's flesh and let seethe them together, and gave him to eat of the same, even as the singer sings --

> "Fish of the wild-wood,
> Worm smooth crawling,
> With wolf-meat mingled,
> They minced for Guttorm;
> Then in the beaker,
> In the wine his mouth knew,
> They set it, still doing
> More deeds of wizards.

Wherefore with the eating of this meat he grew so wild and eager, and with all things about him, and with the heavy words of Grimhild, that he gave his word to do the deed; and mighty honour they promised him in reward thereof.

But of these evil wiles naught at all knew Sigurd, for he might not deal with his shapen fate, nor the measure of his life-days, neither deemed he that he was worthy such things at their hands.

So Guttorm went in to Sigurd the next morning as he lay upon his bed, yet durst

he not do aught against him, but shrank back out again; yea, and even so he fared
a second time, for so bright and eager were the eyes of Sigurd that few durst look
upon him. But the third time he went in, and there lay Sigurd asleep; then Guttorm
drew his sword and thrust Sigurd through in such wise that the sword point smote
into the bed beneath him; then Sigurd awoke with that wound, and Guttorm gat
him unto the door; but therewith Sigurd caught up the sword Gram, and cast it after
him, and it smote him on the back, and struck him asunder in the midst, so that the
feet of him fell one way, and the head and hands back into the chamber.

Now Gudrun lay asleep on Sigurd's bosom, but she woke up unto woe that may
not be told of, all swimming in the blood of him, and in such wise did she bewail her
with weeping and words of sorrow, that Sigurd rose up on the bolster, and spake.

"Weep not," said he, "for thy brothers live for thy delight; but a young son have
I, too young to be ware of his foes; and an ill turn have these played against their
own fortune; for never will they get a mightier brother-in-law to ride abroad with
them; nay, nor a better son to their sister, than this one, if he may grow to man's
estate. Lo, now is that come to pass which was foretold me long ago, but from mine
eyes has it been hidden, for none may fight against his fate and prevail. Behold this
has Brynhild brought to pass, even she who loves me before all men; but this may I
swear, that never have I wrought ill to Gunnar, but rather have ever held fast to my
oath with him, nor was I ever too much a friend to his wife. And now if I had been
forewarned, and had been afoot with my weapons, then should many a man have
lost his life or ever I had fallen, and all those brethren should have been slain, and
a harder work would the slaying of me have been than the slaying of the mightiest
bull or the mightiest boar of the wild-wood."

And even therewithal life left the King; but Gudrun moaned and drew a weary
breath, and Brynhild heard it and laughed when she heard her moaning.

Then said Gunnar, "Thou laughest not because thy heart-roots are gladdened,
or else why doth thy visage wax so wan? Sure an evil creature thou art; most like
thou art nigh to thy death! Lo now, how meet would it be for thee to behold
thy brother Atli slain before thine eyes, and that thou shouldst stand over him
dead; whereas we must needs now stand over our brother-in-law in such a case our
brother-in-law and our brother's bane."

She answered, "None need mock at the measure of slaughter being unfulfilled;

yet heedeth not Atli your wrath or your threats; yea, he shall live longer than ye, and be a mightier man."

Hogni spake and said, "Now hath come to pass the soothsaying of Brynhild; an ill work not to be atoned for."

And Gudrun said, "My kinsmen have slain my husband; but ye, when ye next ride to the war and are come into the battle, then shall ye look about and see that Sigurd is neither on the fight hand nor the left, and ye shall know that he was your good-hap and your strength; and if he had lived and had sons, then should ye have been strengthened by his offspring and his kin."

CHAPTER XXXI. Of the Lamentation of Gudrun over Sigurd's dead, as it is told told in ancient Songs. (1)

Gudrun of old days
Drew near to dying
As she sat in sorrow
Over Sigurd;
Yet she sighed not
Nor smote hand on hand,
Nor wailed she aught
As other women.

Then went earls to her.
Full of all wisdom,
Fain help to deal
To her dreadful heart:
Hushed was Gudrun
Of wail, or greeting,
But with a heavy woe
Was her heart a-breaking.

Bright and fair
Sat the great earls' brides,
Gold arrayed
Before Gudrun;
Each told the tale
Of her great trouble,

The bitterest bale
She erst abode.

Then spake Giaflaug,
Giuki's sister:
"Lo upon earth
I live most loveless
Who of five mates
Must see the ending,
Of daughters twain
And three sisters,
Of brethren eight,
And abide behind lonely."

Naught gat Gudrun
Of wail and greeting,
So heavy was she
For her dead husband,
So dreadful-hearted
For the King laid dead there.

Then spake Herborg
Queen of Hunland --
"Crueller tale
Have I to tell of,
Of my seven sons
Down in the Southlands,
And the eighth man, my mate,
Felled in the death-mead.

"Father and mother,
And four brothers,
On the wide sea

The winds and death played with;
The billows beat
On the bulwark boards.

"Alone must I sing o'er them,
Alone must I array them,
Alone must my hands deal with
Their departing;
And all this was
In one season's wearing,
And none was left
For love or solace.

"Then was I bound
A prey of the battle,
When that same season
Wore to its ending;
As a tiring may
Must I bind the shoon
Of the duke's high dame,
Every day at dawning.

"From her jealous hate
Gat I heavy mocking,
Cruel lashes
She laid upon me,
Never met I
Better master
Or mistress worser
In all the wide world."

Naught gat Gudrun
Of wail or greeting,

So heavy was she
For her dead husband,
So dreadful-hearted
For the King laid dead there.

Then spake Gullrond,
Giuki's daughter --
"O foster-mother,
Wise as thou mayst be,
Naught canst thou better
The young wife's bale."
And she bade uncover
The dead King's corpse.

She swept the sheet
Away from Sigurd,
And turned his cheek
Towards his wife's knees --
"Look on thy loved one
Lay lips to his lips,
E'en as thou wert clinging
To thy king alive yet!"

Once looked Gudrun --
One look only,
And saw her lord's locks
Lying all bloody,
The great man's eyes
Glazed and deadly,
And his heart's bulwark
Broken by sword-edge.

Back then sank Gudrun,

Back on the bolster,
Loosed was her head array,
Red did her cheeks grow,
And the rain-drops ran
Down over her knees.

Then wept Gudrun,
Giuki's daughter,
So that the tears flowed
Through the pillow;
As the geese withal
That were in the homefield,
The fair fowls the may owned,
Fell a-screaming.

Then spake Gullrond,
Giuki's daughter --
"Surely knew I
No love like your love
Among all men,
On the mould abiding;
Naught wouldst thou joy in
Without or within doors,
O my sister,
Save beside Sigurd."

Then spake Gudrun,
Giuki's daughter --
"Such was my Sigurd
Among the sons of Giuki,
As is the king leek
O'er the low grass waxing,
Or a bright stone

Strung on band,
Or a pearl of price
On a prince's brow.

"Once was I counted
By the king's warriors
Higher than any
Of Herjan's mays;
Now am I as little
As the leaf may be,
Amid wind-swept wood
Now when dead he lieth.

I miss from my seat,
I miss from my bed,
My darling of sweet speech.
Wrought the sons of Giuki,
Wrought the sons of Giuki,
This sore sorrow,
Yea, for their sister,
Most sore sorrow.

"So may your lands
Lie waste on all sides,
As ye have broken
Your bounden oaths!
Ne'er shalt thou, Gunnar,
The gold have joy of;
The dear-bought rings
Shall drag thee to death,
Whereon thou swarest
Oath unto Sigurd.

Ah, in the days by-gone
Great mirth in the homefield
When my Sigurd
Set saddle on Grani,
And they went their ways
For the wooing of Brynhild!
An ill day, an ill woman,
And most ill hap!"

Then spake Brynhild,
Budli's daughter --
"May the woman lack
Both love and children,
Who gained greeting
For thee, O Gudrun!
Who gave thee this morning
Many words!"

Then spake Gullrond,
Giuki's daughter --
"Hold peace of such words
Thou hated of all folk!
The bane of brave men
Hast thou been ever,
All waves of ill
Wash over thy mind,
To seven great kings
Hast thou been a sore sorrow,
And the death of good will
To wives and women."

Then spake Brynhild,
Budli's daughter --

"None but Atli
Brought bale upon us,
My very brother
Born of Budli.

When we saw in the hall
Of the Hunnish people
The gold a-gleaming
On the kingly Giukings;
I have paid for that faring
Oft and Full,
And for the sight
That then I saw."

By a pillar she stood
And strained its wood to her;
From the eyes of Brynhild,
Budli's daughter,
Flashed out fire,
And she snorted forth venom,
As the sore wounds she gazed on
Of the dead-slain Sigurd.

ENDNOTES:

(1) This chapter is the Eddaic poem, called the first Lay of
   Gudrun, inserted here by the translators.

CHAPTER XXXII. Of the Ending of Brynhild.

And now none might know for what cause Brynhild must bewail with weeping for what she had prayed for with laughter: but she spake -- "Such a dream I had, Gunnar, as that my bed was acold, and that thou didst ride into the hands of thy foes: lo now, ill shall it go with thee and all thy kin, O ye breakers of oaths; for on the day thou slayedst him, dimly didst thou remember how thou didst blend thy blood with the blood of Sigurd, and with an ill reward hast thou rewarded him for all that he did well to thee; whereas he gave unto thee to be the mightiest of men; and well was it proven how fast he held to his oath sworn, when he came to me and laid betwixt us the sharp-edged sword that in venom had been made hard. All too soon did ye fall to working wrong against him and against me, whenas I abode at home with my father, and had all that I would, and had no will that any one of you should be any of mine, as ye rode into our garth, ye three kings together; but then Atli led me apart privily, and asked me if I would not have him who rode Grani; yea, a man nowise like unto you; but in those days I plighted myself to the son of King Sigmund and no other; and lo, now, no better shall ye fare for the death of me."

Then rose up Gunnar, and laid his arms about her neck, and besought her to live and have wealth from him; and all others in likewise letted her from dying; but she thrust them all from her, and said that it was not the part of any to let her in that which was her will.

Then Gunnar called to Hogni, and prayed him for counsel, and bade him go to her, and see if he might perchance soften her dreadful heart, saying withal, that now they had need enough on their hands in the slaking of her grief, till time might get over.

But Hogni answered, "Nay, let no man hinder her from dying; for no gain will she be to us, nor has she been gainsome since she came hither!

Now she bade bring forth much gold, and bade all those come thither who would have wealth: then she caught up a sword, and thrust it under her armpit, and sank aside upon the pillows, and said, "Come, take gold whoso will!"

But all held their peace, and she said, "Take the gold, and be glad thereof!"

And therewith she spake unto Gunnar, "Now for a little while will I tell of that which shall come to pass hereafter; for speedily shall ye be at one again with Gudrun by the rede of Grimhild the Wise-wife; and the daughter of Gudrun and Sigurd shall be called Swanhild, the fairest of all women born. Gudrun shall be given to Atli, yet not with her good will. Thou shalt be fain to get Oddrun, but that shall Atli forbid thee; but privily shall ye meet, and much shall she love thee. Atli shall bewray thee, and cast thee into a worm-close, and thereafter shall Atli and his Sons be slain, and Gudrun shall be their slayer; and afterwards shall the great waves bear her to the burg of King Jonakr, to whom she shall bear sons of great fame: Swanhild shall be sent from the land and given to King Jormunrek; and her shall bite the rede of Bikki, and therewithal is the kin of you clean gone; and more sorrow therewith for Gudrun.

"And now I pray thee, Gunnar, one last boon. -- Let make a great bale on the plain meads for all of us; for me and for Sigurd, and for those who were slain with him, and let that be covered over with cloth dyed red by the folk of the Gauls, (1) and burn me thereon on one side of the King of the Huns, and on the other those men of mine, two at the head and two at the feet, and two hawks withal; and even so is all shared equally; and lay there betwixt us a drawn sword, as in the other days when we twain stepped into one bed together; and then may we have the name of man and wife, nor shall the door swing to at the heel of him as I go behind him. Nor shall that be a niggard company if there follow him those five bond-women and eight bondmen, whom my father gave me, and those burn there withal who were slain with Sigurd.

"Now more yet would I say, but for my wounds, but my life-breath flits; the wounds open, -- yet have I said sooth."

Now is the dead corpse of Sigurd arrayed in olden wise, and a mighty bale is raised, and when it was somewhat kindled, there was laid thereon the dead corpse of Sigurd Fafnir's-bane, and his son of three winters whom Brynhild had let slay, and Guttorm withal; and when the bale was all ablaze, thereunto was Brynhild borne out, when she had spoken with her bower-maidens, and bid them take the gold that she would give; and then died Brynhild, and was burned there by the side of Sigurd, and thus their life- days ended.

ENDNOTES:

(1) The original has "raudu manna blodi", red-dyed in the blood
     of men; the Sagaman's original error in dealing with the
     word "Valaript" in the corresponding passage of the short
     lay of Sigurd. -- Tr.

CHAPTER XXXIII. Gudrun wedded to Alii.

Now so it is, that whoso heareth these tidings sayeth, that no such an one as was Sigurd was left behind him in the world, nor ever was such a man brought forth because of all the worth of him, nor may his name ever minish by eld in the Dutch Tongue nor in all the Northern Lands, while the world standeth fast.

The story tells that, on a day, as Gudrun sat in her bower, she fell to saying, "Better was life in those days when I had Sigurd; he who was far above other men as gold is above iron, or the leek over other grass of the field, or the hart over other wild things; until my brethren begrudged me such a man, the first and best of all men; and so they might not sleep or they had slain him. Huge clamour made Grani when he saw his master and lord sore wounded, and then I spoke to him even as with a man, but he fell drooping down to the earth, for he knew that Sigurd was slain."

Thereafter Gudrun gat her gone into the wild woods, and heard on all ways round about her the howling of wolves, and deemed death a merrier thing than life. Then she went till she came to the hall of King Alf, and sat there in Denmark with Thora, the daughter of Hakon, for seven seasons, and abode with good welcome. And she set forth her needlework before her and did thereinto many deeds and great, and fair plays after the fashion of those days, swords and byrnies, and all the gear of kings, and the ship of King Sigmund sailing along the land; yea, and they wrought there how they fought, Sigar and Siggeir, south in Fion. Such was their disport; and now Gudrun was somewhat solaced of her grief.

So Grimhild comes to hear where Gudrun has take up her abode, and she calls her sons to talk with her, and asks whether they will make atonement to Gudrun for her son and her husband, and said that it was but meet and right to do so.

Then Gunnar spake, and said that he would atone for her sorrows with gold.

So they send for their friends, and array their horses, their helms, and their shields, and their byrnies, and all their war- gear; and their journey was furnished forth in the noblest wise, and no champion who was of the great men might abide at home; and their horses were clad in mail-coats, and every knight of them had his helm done over with gold or with silver.

Grimhild was of their company, for she said that their errand would never be brought fairly to pass if she sat at home.

There were well five hundred men, and noble men rode with them. There was Waldemar of Denmark, and Eymod and Jarisleif withal. So they went into the hall of King Alf, and there abode them the Longbeards and Franks, and Saxons: they fared with all their war- gear, and had over them red fur-coats. Even as the song says --

> "Byrnies short cut,
> Strong helms hammered,
> Girt with good swords,
> Red hair gleaming."

They were fain to choose good gifts for their sister, and spake softly to her, but in none of them would she trow. Then Gunnar brought unto her a drink mingled with hurtful things, and this she must needs drink, and with the king thereof she had no more memory of their guilt against her.

But in that drink was blended the might of the earth and the sea with the blood of her son; and in that horn were all letters cut and reddened with blood, as is said hereunder --

> "On the horn's face were there
> All the kin of letters
> Cut aright and reddened,
> How should I rede them rightly?
> The ling-fish long
> Of the land of Hadding,

Wheat-ears unshorn,
And wild things' inwards.

In that beer were mingled
Many ills together,
Blood of all the wood
And brown-burnt acorns,
The black dew of the hearth,
The God-doomed dead beast's inwards,
And the swine's liver sodden
Because all wrongs that deadens.

And so now, when their hearts are-brought anigh to each other, great cheer they made: then came Grimhild to Gudrun, and spake.

"All hail to thee, daughter! I give thee gold and all kinds of good things to take to thee after thy father, dear bought rings and bed-gear of the maids of the Huns, the most courteous and well dight of all women; and thus is thy husband atoned for: and thereafter shalt thou be given to Atli, the mighty king, and be mistress of all his might. Cast not all thy friends aside for one man's sake, but do according to our bidding."

Gudrun answers, "Never will I wed Atli the King; unseemly it is for us to get offspring betwixt us."

Grimhild says, "Nourish not thy wrath; it shall be to thee as if Sigurd and Sigmund were alive when thou hast borne sons."

Gudrun says, "I cannot take my heart from thoughts of him, for he was the first of all men."

Grimhild says, "So it is shapen that thou must have this king and none else."

Says Gudrun, "Give not this man to me, for an evil thing shall come upon thy kin from him, and to his own sons shall he deal evil, and be rewarded with a grim revenge thereafter."

Then waxed Grimhild fell at those words, and spake, "Do even as we bid thee, and take therefore great honour, and our friendship, and the steads withal called Vinbjorg and Valbjorg."

And such might was in the words of her, that even so must it come to pass.

Then Gudrun spake, "Thus then must it needs befall, howsoever against the will of me, and for little joy shall it be and for great grief."

Then men leaped on their horses, and their women were set in wains. So they fared four days a-riding and other four a-shipboard, and yet four more again by land and road, till at the last they came to a certain high-built hall; then came to meet Gudrun many folk thronging; and an exceedingly goodly feast was there made, even as the word had gone between either kin, and it passed forth in most proud and stately wise. And at that feast drinks Atli his bridal with Gudrun, but never did her heart laugh on him, and little sweet and kind was their life together.

CHAPTER XXXIV. Atli bids the Giukings to him.

Now tells the tale that on a night King Atli woke from sleep and spake to Gudrun -- "Medreamed," said he, "that thou didst thrust me through with a sword." Then Gudrun areded the dream, and said that it betokened fire, whenas folk dreamed of iron. "It befalls of thy pride belike, in that thou deemest thyself the first of men,"

Atli said, "Moreover I dreamed that here waxed two sorb-tree (1) saplings, and fain I was that they should have no scathe of me; then these were riven up by the roots and reddened with blood, and borne to the bench, and I was bidden eat thereof.

"Yea, yet again I dreamed that two hawks flew from my hand hungry and unfed, and fared to hell, and meseemed their hearts were mingled with honey, and that I ate thereof.

"And then again I dreamed that two fair whelps lay before me yelling aloud, and that the flesh of them I ate, though my will went not with the eating."

Gudrun says, "Nowise good are these dreams, yet shall they come to pass; surely thy sons are nigh to death, and many heavy things shall fall upon us."

"Yet again I dreamed," said he, "and methought I lay in a bath, and folk took counsel to slay me."

Now these things wear away with time, but in nowise was their life together fond.

Now falls Atli to thinking of where may be gotten that plenteous gold which Sigurd had owned, but King Gunnar and his brethren were lords thereof now.

Atli was a great king and mighty, wise, and a lord of many men; and now he falls to counsel with his folk as to the ways of them. He wotted well that Gunnar and his brethren had more wealth than any others might have, and so he falls to the rede of sending men to them, and bidding them to a great feast, and honouring them in diverse wise, and the chief of those messengers was hight Vingi.

Now the queen wots of their conspiring, and misdoubts her that this would mean some beguiling of her brethren: so she cut runes, and took a gold ring, and knit therein a wolf's hair, and gave it into the hands of the king's messengers.

Thereafter they go their ways according to the king's bidding: and or ever they came aland Vingi beheld the runes, and turned them about in such wise as if Gudrun prayed her brethren in her runes to go meet King Atli.

Thereafter they came to the hall of King Gunnar, and had good welcome at his hands, and great fires were made for them, and in great joyance they drank of the best of drink.

Then spake Vingi, "King Atli sends me hither, and is fain that ye go to his house and home in all glory, and take of him exceeding honours, helms and shields, swords and byrnies, gold and goodly raiment, horses, hosts of war, and great and wide lands, for, saith he, he is fainest of all things to bestow his realm and lordship upon you."

Then Gunnar turned his head aside, and spoke to Hogni --

"In what wise shall we take this bidding? Might and wealth he bids us take; but no kings know I who have so much gold as we have, whereas we have all the hoard which lay once on Gnitaheath; and great are our chambers, and full of gold, and weapons for smiting, and all kinds of raiment of war, and well I wot that amidst all men my horse is the best, and my sword the sharpest and my gold the most glorious."

Hogni answers, "A marvel is it to me of his bidding, for seldom hath he done in such a wise, and ill counselled will it be to wend to him; lo now, when I saw those dear-bought things the king sends us I wondered to behold a wolfs hair knit to a certain gold ring; belike Gudrun deems him to be minded as a wolf towards us, and will have naught of our faring."

But withal Vingi shows him the runes which he said Gudrun had sent.

Now the most of folk go to bed, but these drank on still with certain others; and Kostbera, the wife of Hogni, the fairest of women, came to them, and looked on the runes.

But the wife of Gunnar was Glaumvor, a great hearted wife.

So these twain poured out, and the kings drank and were exceeding drunken, and Vingi notes it, and says --

"Naught may I hide that King Atli is heavy of foot and over-old for the warding of his realm; but his sons are young and of no account: now will he give you rule over his realms while they are yet thus young, and most fain will he be that ye have the joy thereof before all others."

Now so it befell both that Gunnar was drunk, and that dominion was held out to him, nor might he work against the fate shapen for him; so he gave his word to go, and tells Hogni his brother thereof.

But he answered, "Thy word given must even stand now, nor will I fail to follow thee, but most loth am I to journey."

ENDNOTES:

(1) Service-tree; "pyrus sorbus domestica", or "p. s.
    tormentalis.

CHAPTER XXXV. The Dreams of the Wives of the Giukings.

So when men had drunk their fill, they fared to sleep; then falls Kostbera to beholding the runes, and spelling over the letters, and sees that beneath were other things cut, and that the runes are guileful, yet because of her wisdom she had skill to read them aright. So then she goes to bed by her husband; but when they awoke, she spake unto Hogni --

"Thou art minded to wend away from home -- ill-counselled is that; abide till another time! Scarce a keen reader of runes art thou, if thou deemest thou hast beheld in them the bidding of thy sister to this journey: lo, I read them the runes, and had marvel of so wise a woman as Gudrun is, that she should have miscut them; but that which lieth underneath beareth your bane with it, -- yea, either she lacked a letter, or others have dealt guilefully with the runes.

"And now hearken to my dream; for therein methought there fell in upon us here a river exceeding strong, and brake up the timbers of the hall."

He answered, "Full oft are ye evil of mind, ye women, but for me, I was not made in such wise as to meet men with evil who deserve no evil; belike he will give us good welcome."

She answered, "Well, the thing must ye yourselves prove, but no friendship follows this bidding: -- but yet again I dreamed that another river fell in here with a great and grimly rush, and tore up the dais of the hall, and brake the legs of both you brethren; surely that betokeneth somewhat."

He answers, "Meadows along our way, whereas thou didst dream of the river; for when we go through the meadows, plentifully doth the seeds of the hay hang about our legs."

"Again I dreamed," she says, "that thy cloak was afire, and that the flame blazed up above the hall."

Says he, "Well, I wot what that shall betoken; here lieth my fair-dyed raiment, and it shall burn and blaze, whereas thou dreamedst of the cloak."

"Methought a bear came in," she says, "and brake up the king's high-seat, and shook his paws in such a wise that we were all adrad thereat, and he gat us all together into the mouth of him, so that we might avail us naught, and thereof fell great horror on us."

He answered, "Some great storm will befall, whereas thou hadst a white bear in thy mind."

"An erne methought came in," she says, "and swept adown the hall, and drenched me and all of us with blood, and ill shall that betoken, for methought it was the double of King Atli."

He answered, "Full oft do we slaughter beasts freely, and smite down great neat for our cheer, and the dream of the erne has but to do with oxen; yea, Atli is heart-whole toward us."

And therewithal they cease this talk.

CHAPTER XXXVI. Of the Journey of the Giukings to King Atli.

Now tells the tale of Gunnar, that in the same wise it fared with him; for when they awoke, Glaumvor his wife told him many dreams which seemed to her like to betoken guile coming; but Gunnar areded them all in other wise.

"This was one of them," said she; "methought a bloody sword was borne into the hall here, wherewith thou wert thrust through, and at either end of that wolves howled."

The king answered, "Our dogs shall bite me belike; blood-stained weapons oft betoken dogs' snappings."

She said, "Yet again I dreamed -- that women came in, heavy and drooping, and chose thee for their mate; may-happen these would be thy fateful women."

He answered, "Hard to arede is this, and none may set aside the fated measure of his days, nor is it unlike that my time is short." (1)

So in the morning they arose, and were minded for the journey, but some letted them herein.

Then cried Gunnar to the man who is called Fjornir --

"Arise, and give us to drink goodly wine from great tuns, because may happen this shall be very last of all our feasts; belike if we die the old wolf shall come by the gold, and that bear shall nowise spare the bite of his war-tusks."

Then all the folk of his household brought them on their way weeping.

The son of Hogni said --

"Fare ye well with merry tide."

The more part of their folk were left behind; Solar and Gnoevar, the sons of Hogni, fared with them, and a great champion, named Orkning, who was the brother of Kostbera.

So folk followed them down to the ships, and all fetted them of their journey, but attained to naught therein.

Then spake Glaumvor, and said --

"O Vingi, most like that great ill hap will come of thy coming, and mighty and evil things shall betide in thy travelling."

He answered, "Hearken to my answer; that I lie not aught: and may the high gallows and all things of grame have me, if I lie one word!"

Then cried Kostbera, "Fare ye well with merry days."

And Hogni answered, "Be glad of heart, howsoever it may fare with us!"

And therewith they parted, each to their own fate. Then away they rowed, so hard and fast, that well-nigh the half of the keel slipped away from the ship, and so hard they laid on to the oars that thole and gunwale brake.

But when they came aland they made their ship fast, and then they rode awhile on their noble steeds through the murk wild-wood.

And now they behold the king's army, and huge uproar, and the clatter of weapons they hear from thence; and they see there a mighty host of men, and the manifold array of them, even as they wrought there: and all the gates of the burg were full of men.

So they rode up to the burg, and the gates thereof were shut; then Hogni brake open the gates, and therewith they ride into the burg.

Then spake Vingi, "Well might ye have left this deed undone; go to now, bide ye here while I go seek your gallows-tree! Softly and sweetly I base you hither, but an evil thing abode thereunder; short while to bide ere ye are tied up to that same tree!"

Hogni answered, "None the more shall we waver for that cause; for little methinks have we shrunk aback whenas men fell to fight; and naught shall it avail thee to make us afeard, -- and for an ill fate hast thou wrought."

And therewith they cast him down to earth, and smote him with their axe-hammers till he died.

ENDNOTES:

(1) Parallel beliefs to those in the preceding chapters, and
    elsewhere in this book, as to spells, dreams, drinks, etc.,
    among the English people may be found in "Leechdoms,
    Wortcunning, and Starcraft of the Anglo-Saxons; being a
    collection of Documents illustrating the History of Science
    in this Country before the Norman Conquest". Ed: Rev. T. O.
    Cockayne, M.A. (3 vols.) Longmans, London, 1864, 8vo.

CHAPTER XXXVII. The Battle in
the Burg of King Atli.

Then they rode unto the king's hall, and King Atli arrayed his host for battle, and the ranks were so set forth that a certain wall there was betwixt them and the brethren. "Welcome hither," said he. "Deliver unto me that plenteous gold which is mine of right; even the wealth which Sigurd once owned, and which is now Gudrun's of right."

Gunnar answered, "Never gettest thou that wealth; and men of might must thou meet here, or ever we lay by life if thou wilt deal with us in battle; ah, belike thou settest forth this feast like a great man, and wouldst not hold thine hand from erne and wolf!"

"Long ago I had it in my mind," said Atli, to take the lives of you, and be lord of the gold, and reward you for that deed of shame, wherein ye beguiled the best of all your affinity; but now shall I revenge him."

Hogni answered, "Little will it avail to lie long brooding over that rede, leaving the work undone."

And therewith they fell to hard fighting, at the first brunt with shot.

But therewithal came the tidings to Gudrun, and when she heard thereof she grew exceeding wroth, and cast her mantle from her, and ran out and greeted those new-comers, and kissed her brethren, and showed them all love, -- and the last of all greetings was that betwixt them.

Then said she, "I thought I had set forth counsel whereby ye should not come hither, but none may deal with his shapen fate." And withal she said, "Will it avail aught to seek for peace?"

But stoutly and grimly they said nay thereto. So she sees that the game goeth sorely against her brethren, and she gathers to her great stoutness of heart, and does on her a mail-coat and takes to her a sword, and fights by her brethren, and goes as far forward as the bravest of man-folk; and all spoke in one wise that never saw any fairer defence than in her.

Now the men fell thick, and far before all others was the fighting of those brethren, and the battle endured a long while unto midday; Gunnar and Hogni went right through the folk of Atli, and so tells the tale that all the mead ran red with blood; the sons of Hogni withal set on stoutly.

Then spake Atli the king, "A fair host and a great have we, and mighty champions withal, and yet have many of us fallen, and but evil am I apaid in that nineteen of my champions are slain, and but left six alive."

And therewithal was there a lull in the battle.

Then spake Atli the king, "Four brethren were we, and now am I left alone; great affinity I gat to me, and deemed my fortune well sped thereby; a wife I had, fair and wise, high of mind, and great of heart; but no joyance may I have of her wisdom, for little peace is betwixt us, -- but ye -- ye have slain many of my kin, and beguiled me of realm and riches, and for the greatest of all woes have slain my sister withal."

Quoth Hogni, "Why babblest thou thus? Thou wert the first to break the peace. Thou didst take my kinswoman and pine her to death by hunger, and didst murder her, and take her wealth; an ugly deed for a king! -- meet for mocking and laughter I deem it, that thou must needs make long tale of thy woes; rather will I give thanks to the Gods that thou fallest into ill."

CHAPTER XXXVIII. Of the slaying of the Giukings.

Now King Atli eggs on his folk to set on fiercely, and eagerly they fight; but the Giukings fell on so hard that King Atli gave back into the hall, and within doors was the fight, and fierce beyond all fights. That battle was the death of many a man, but such was the ending thereof, that there fell all the folk of those brethren, and they twain alone stood up on their feet, and yet many more must fare to hell first before their weapons.

And now they fell on Gunnar the king, and because of the host of men that set on him was hand laid on him, and he was cast into fetters; afterwards fought Hogni, with the stoutest heart and the greatest manlihood; and he felled to earth twenty of the stoutest of the champions of King Atli, and many he thrust into the fire that burnt amidst the hall, and all were of one accord that such a man might scarce be seen; yet in the end was he borne down by many and taken.

Then said King Atli, "A marvellous thing how many men have gone their ways before him! Cut the heart from out of him, and let that be his bane!"

Hogni said, "Do according to thy will; merrily will I abide whatso thou writ do against me; and thou shalt see that my heart is not adrad, for hard matters have I made trial of ere now, and all things that may try a man was I fain to bear, whiles yet I was unhurt; but now sorely am I hurt, and thou alone henceforth will bear mastery in our dealings together."

Then spake a counsellor of King Atli, "Better rede I see thereto; take we the thrall Hjalli, and give respite to Hogni; for this thrall is made to die, since the longer he lives the less worth shall he be."

The thrall hearkened, and cried out aloft, and fled away anywhither where he might hope for shelter, crying out that a hard portion was his because of their strife and wild doings, and an ill day for him whereon he must be dragged to death from his sweet life and his swine-keeping. But they caught him, and turned a knife against him, and he yelled and screamed or ever he felt the point thereof.

Then in such wise spake Hogni as a man seldom speaketh who is fallen into hard need, for he prayed for the thrall's life, and said that these shrieks he could not away with, and that it were a lesser matter to him to play out the play to the end; and therewithal the thrall gat his life as for that time: but Gunnar and Hogni are both laid in fetters.

Then spake King Atli with Gunnar the king, and bade him tell out concerning the gold, and where it was, if he would have his life.

But he answered, "Nay, first will I behold the bloody heart of Hogni, my brother."

So now they caught hold of the thrall again, and cut the heart from out of him, and bore it unto King Gunnar, but he said --

"The faint heart of Hjalli may ye here behold, little like the proud heart of Hogni, for as much as it trembleth now more by the half it trembled whenas it lay in the breast of him."

So now they fell on Hogni even as Atli urged them, and cut the heart from out of him, but such was the might of his manhood, that he laughed while he abode that torment, and all wondered at his worth, and in perpetual memory is it held sithence. (1)

Then they showed it to Gunnar, and he said --

"The mighty heart of Hogni, little like the faint heart of Hjalli, for little as it trembleth now, less it trembled whenas in his breast it lay! But now, O Atli, even as we die so shalt thou die; and lo, I alone wot where the gold is, nor shall Hogni be to tell thereof now; to and fro played the matter in my mind whiles we both lived, but now have I myself determined for myself, and the Rhine river shall rule over the gold, rather than that the Huns shall bear it on the hands of them."

Then said King Atli, "Have away the bondsman;" and so they did.

But Gudrun called to her men, and came to Atli, and said --

"May it fare ill with thee now and from henceforth, even as thou hast ill held to thy word with me!"

So Gunnar was cast into a worm-close, and many worms abode him there, and his hands were fast bound; but Gudrun sent him a harp, and in such wise did he set

forth his craft, that wisely he smote the harp, smiting it with his foes, and so excel-
lently well he played, that few deemed they had heard such playing, even when the
hand had done it. And with such might and power he played, that all worms fell
asleep in the end, save one adder only, great and evil of aspect, that crept unto him
and thrust its sting into him until it smote his heart; and in such wise with great
hardihood he ended his life days.

ENDNOTES:

(1) Since ("sidh", after, and "dham", that.).

CHAPTER XXXIX. The End of Atli and his Kin and Folk.

Now thought Atli the King that he had gained a mighty victory, and spake to Gudrun even as mocking her greatly, or as making himself great before her. "Gudrun," saith he, "thus hast thou lost thy brethren, and thy very self hast brought it about."

She answers, "In good liking livest thou, whereas thou thrustest these slayings before me, but mayhappen thou wilt rue it, when thou hast tried what is to come hereafter; and of all I have, the longest-lived matter shall be the memory of thy cruel heart, nor shall it go well with thee whiles I live."

He answered and said, "Let there be peace betwixt us; I will atone for thy brethren with gold and dear-bought things, even as thy heart may wish."

She answers, "Hard for a long while have I been in our dealings together, and now I say, that while Hogni was yet alive thou mightest have brought it to pass; but now mayest thou never atone for my brethren in my heart; yet oft must we women be overborne by the might of you men; and now are all my kindred dead and gone, and thou alone art left to rule over me: wherefore now this is my counsel that we make a great feast; wherein I will hold the funeral of my brother and of thy kindred withal."

In such wise did she make herself soft and kind in words, though far other things forsooth lay thereunder, but he hearkened to her gladly, and trusted in her words, whereas she made herself sweet of speech.

So Gudrun held the funeral feast for her brethren, and King Atli for his men, and exceeding proud and great was this feast.

But Gudrun forgat not her woe, but brooded over it, how she might work some mighty shame against the king; and at nightfall she took to her the sons of King Atli and her as they played about the floor; the younglings waxed heavy of cheer, and asked what she would with them.

"Ask me not," she said; "ye shall die, the twain of you!"

Then they answered, "Thou mayest do with thy children even as thou wilt, nor shall any hinder thee, but shame there is to thee in the doing of this deed."

Yet for all that she cut the throats of them.

Then the king asked where his sons were, and Gudrun answered, "I will tell thee, and gladden thine heart by the telling; lo now, thou didst make a great woe spring up for me in the slaying of my brethren; now hearken and hear my rede and my deed; thou hast lost thy sons, and their heads are become beakers on the board here, and thou thyself hast drunken the blood of them blended with wine; and their hearts I took and roasted them on a spit, and thou hast eaten thereof."

King Atli answered, "Grim art thou in that thou hast murdered thy sons, and given me their flesh to eat, and little space passes betwixt ill deed of thine and ill deed."

Gudrun said, "My heart is set on the doing to thee of as great shame as may be; never shall the measure ill be of full to such a king as thou art."

The king said, "Worser deeds hast thou done than men have to tell of, and great unwisdom is there in such fearful redes; most meet art thou to be burned on bale when thou hast first been smitten to death with stones, for in such wise wouldst thou have what thou hast gone a weary way to seek."

She answered, "Thine own death thou foretellest, but another death is fated for me."

And many other words they spake in their wrath.

Now Hogni had a son left alive, hight Niblung, and great wrath of heart he bare against King Atli; and he did Gudrun to wit that he would avenge his father. And she took his words well, and they fell to counsel together thereover, and she said it would be great goodhap if it might be brought about.

So on a night, when the king had drunken, he gat him in bed, and when he was laid asleep, thither to him came Gudrun and the son of Hogni.

Gudrun took a sword and thrust it through the breast of King Atli, and they both of them set their hands to the deed, both she and the son of Hogni.

Then Atli the king awoke with the wound, and cried out; "No need of binding or salving here! -- who art thou who hast done the deed?"

Gudrun says, "Somewhat have I, Gudrun, wrought therein, and somewhat withal the son of Hogni."

Atli said, "Ill it beseemed to thee to do this, though somewhat of wrong was between us; for thou wert wedded to me by the rede of thy kin, and dower paid I for thee; yea, thirty goodly knights, and seemly maidens, and many men besides; and yet wert thou not content, but if thou should rule over the lands King Budli owned: and thy mother-in-law full oft thou lettest sit a-weeping."

Gudrun said, "Many false words hast thou spoken, and of naught I account them; oft, indeed, was I fell of mood, but much didst thou add thereto. Full oft in this thy house did frays befall, and kin fought kin, and friend fought friend, and made themselves big one against the other; better days had I whenas I abode with Sigurd, when we slew kings, and took their wealth to us, but gave peace to whomso would, and the great men laid themselves under our hands, and might we gave to him of them who would have it; then I lost him, and a little thing was it that I should bear a widow's name, but the greatest of griefs that I should come to thee -- I who had aforetime the noblest of all kings, while for thee, thou never barest out of the battle aught but the worser lot."

King Atli answered, "Naught true are thy words, nor will this our speech better the lot of either of us, for all is fallen now to naught; but now do to me in seemly wise, and array my dead corpse in noble fashion."

"Yea, that will I," she says, "and let make for thee a goodly grave, and build for thee a worthy abiding place of stone, and wrap thee in fair linen, and care for all that needful is."

So therewithal he died, and she did according to her word: and then they cast fire into the hall.

And when the folk and men of estate awoke amid that dread and trouble, naught would they abide the fire, but smote each the other down, and died in such wise; so there Atli the king, and all his folk, ended their life-days. But Gudrun had no will to live longer after this deed so wrought, but nevertheless her ending day was not yet come upon her.

Now the Volsungs and the Giukings, as folk tell in tale, have been the greatest-hearted and the mightiest of all men, as ye may well behold written in the songs of old time.

But now with the tidings just told were these troubles stayed.

CHAPTER XL. How Gudrun cast herself into the Sea, but was brought ashore again.

Gudrun had a daughter by Sigurd hight Swanhild; she was the fairest of all women, eager-eyed as her father, so that few durst look under the brows of her; and as far did she excel other woman-kind as the sun excels the other lights of heaven.

But on a day went Gudrun down to the sea, and caught up stones in her arms, and went out into the sea, for she had will to end her life. But mighty billows drave her forth along the sea, and by means of their upholding was she borne along till she came at the last to the burg of King Jonakr, a mighty king, and lord of many folk. And he took Gudrun to wife, and their children were Hamdir, and Sorli, and Erp; and there was Swanhild nourished withal.

CHAPTER XLI. Of the Wedding and Slaying of Swanhild.

Jormunrek was the name of a mighty king of those days, and his son was called Randver. Now this king called his son to talk with him, and said, "Thou shalt fair on an errand of mine to King Jonakr, with my counsellor Bikki, for with King Jonakr is nourished Swanhild, the daughter of Sigurd Fafnir's-bane; and I know for sure that she is the fairest may dwelling under the sun of this world; her above all others would I have to my wife, and thou shalt go woo her for me"

Randver answered, "Meet and right, fair lord, that I should go on thine errands."

So the king set forth this journey in seemly wise, and they fare till they come to King Jonakr's abode, and behold Swanhild, and have many thoughts concerning the treasure of her goodliness.

But on a day Randver called the king to talk with him, and said, "Jormunrek the King would fain be thy brother-in-law, for he has heard tell of Swanhild, and his desire it is to have her to wife, nor may it be shown that she may be given to any mightier man than he is one."

The King says, "This is an alliance of great honour, for a man of fame he is."

Gudrun says, "A wavering trust, the trust in luck that change not!"

Yet because of the king's furthering, and all the matters that went herewith, is the wooing accomplished; and Swanhild went to the ship with a goodly company, and sat in the stem beside the king's son.

Then spake Bikki to Randver, "How good and right it were if thou thyself had to wife so lovely a woman rather than the old man there."

Good seemed that word to the heart of the king's son, and he spake to her with sweet words, and she to him like wise.

So they came aland and go unto the king, and Bikki said to him, "Meet and right it is, lord, that thou shouldst know what is befallen, though hard it be to tell of, for the tale must be concerning thy beguiling, whereas thy son has gotten to him the full love of Swanhild, nor is she other than his harlot; but thou, let not the deed be unavenged."

Now many an ill rede had he given the king or this, but of all his ill redes did this sting home the most; and still would the king hearken to all his evil redes; wherefore he, who might nowise still the wrath within him, cried out that Randver should be taken and tied up to the gallows-tree.

And as he was led to the gallows he took his hawk and plucked the feathers from off it, and bade show it to his father; and when the king saw it, then he said, "Now may folk behold that he deemeth my honour to be gone away from me, even as the feathers of this hawk;" and therewith he bade deliver him from the gallows.

But in that while had Bikki wrought his will, and Randver was dead-slain.

Ane, moreover, Bikki spake, "Against none hast thou more wrongs to avenge thee of than against Swanhild; let her die a shameful death."

"Yea," said the king, "we will do after thy counsel."

So she was bound in the gate of the burg, and horse were driven at her to tread her down; but when she opened her eyes wide, then the horses durst not trample her; so when Bikki beheld that, he bade draw a bag over the head of her; and they did so, and therewith she lost her life. (1)

ENDNOTES

(1) In the prose Edda the slaying of Swanhild is a spontaneous and sudden act on the part of the king. As he came back from hunting one day, there sat Swanhild washing her linen, and it came into the king's mind how that she was the cause of all his woe, so he and his men rode over her and slew her. -- Tr.

CHAPTER XLII. Gudrun sends her Sons to avenge Swanhild.

Now Gudrun heard of the slaying of Swanhild, and spake to her sons, "Why sit ye here in peace amid many words, whereas Jormunrek hath slain your sister, and trodden her under foot of horses in shameful wise? No heart ye have in you like to Gunnar or Hogni; verily they would have avenged their kinswoman!"

Hamdir answered, "Little didst thou praise Gunnar and Hogni, whereas they slew Sigurd, and thou wert reddened in the blood of him, and ill were thy brethren avenged by the slaying of thine own sons: yet not so ill a deed were it for us to slay King Jormunrek, and so hard thou pushest on to this that we may naught abide thy hard words."

Gudrun went about laughing now, and gave them to drink from mighty beakers, and thereafter she got for them great byrnies and good, and all other weed (1) of war.

Then spake Hamdir, "Lo now, this is our last parting, for thou shalt hear tidings of us, and drink one grave-ale (2) over us and over Swanhild."

So therewith they went their ways.

But Gudrun went unto her bower, with heart swollen with sorrow, and spake

--

"To three men was I wedded, and first to Sigurd Fafnir's-bane, and he was be-wrayed and slain, and of all griefs was that the greatest grief. Then was I given to King Atli, and so fell was my heart toward him that I slew in the fury of my grief his children and mine. Then gave I myself to the sea, but the billows thereof cast me out aland, and to this king then was I given; then gave I Swanhild away out of the land with mighty wealth; and lo, my next greatest sorrow after Sigurd, for under horses feet was she trodden and slain; but the grimmest and ugliest of woes was the casting of Gunnar into the Worm-close, and the hardest was the cutting of Hogni's heart from him.

"Ah, better would it be if Sigurd came to meet me, and I went my ways with him, for here bideth now behind with me neither son nor daughter to comfort me. Oh, mindest thou not, Sigurd, the words we spoke when we went into one bed together, that thou wouldst come and look on me; yea, even from thine abiding place among the dead?

And thus had the words of her sorrow an end.

ENDNOTE:

(1) Weed (A.S. "weodo"), clothing.
(2) Grave-ale, burial-feast.

CHAPTER XLIII. The Latter End of all the Kin of the Giukings.

Now telleth the tale concerning the sons of Gudrun, that she had arrayed their war-raiment in such wise, that no steel would bite thereon; and she bade them play not with stones or other heavy matters, for that it would be to their scathe if they did so.

And now, as they went on their way, they met Erp, their brother, and asked him in what wise he would help them.

He answered, "Even as hand helps hand, or foot helps foot."

But that they deemed naught at all, and slew him there and then. Then they went their ways, nor was it long or ever Hamdir stumbled, and thrust down his hand to steady himself, and spake therewith --

"Naught but a true thing spake Erp, for now should I have fallen, had not hand been to steady me."

A little after Sorli stumbled, but turned about on his feet, and so stood, and spake --

"Yea now had I fallen, but that I steadied myself with both feet."

And they said they had done evilly with Erp their brother.

But on they fare till they come to the abode of King Jormunrek, and they went up to him and set on him forthwith, and Hamdir cut both hands from him and Sorli both feet. Then spake Hamdir --

"Off were the head if Erp were alive; our brother whom we slew on the way, and found out our deed too late." Even as the Song says, --

"Off were the head
If Erp were alive yet,

Our brother the bold,
Whom we slew by the way,
The well-famed in warfare."

Now in this must they turn away from the words of their mother, whereas they had to deal with stones. For now men fell on them, and they defended themselves in good and manly wise, and were the scathe of many a man, nor would iron bite on them.

But there came thereto a certain man, old of aspect and one-eyed, (1) and he spake --

"No wise men are ye, whereas ye cannot bring these men to their end."

Then the king said, "Give us rede thereto, if thou canst."

He said, "Smite them to the death with stones."

In such wise was it done, for the stones flew thick and fast from every side, and that was the end of their life-days.

And now has come to an end the whole root and stem of the Giukings. (2)

NOW MAY ALL EARLS
BE BETTERED IN MIND,
MAY THE GRIEF OF ALL MAIDENS
EVER BE MINISHED,
FOR THIS TALE OF TROUBLE
SO TOLD TO ITS ENDING.

ENDNOTES:

(1) Odin; he ends the tale as he began it.
(2) "And now," etc., inserted by translators from the prose
     Edda, the stanza at the end from the Whetting of Gudrun.

APPENDIX: EXCERPTS FROM THE POETIC EDDA. PART OF THE SECOND LAY OF HELGI HUNDINGS-BANE (1)

DAG:
Loth am I, sister
Of sorrow to tell the,
For by hard need driven
Have I drawn on the greeting;
This morning fell
In Fetter-grove
The king well deemed
The best in the wide world,
Yea, he who stood
On the necks of the strong."

SIGRUN:
All oaths once sworn
Shall bite thee sore,
The oaths that to Helgi
Once thou swarest
At the bright white
Water of Lightening, (3)
And at the cold rock
That the sea runneth over.

May the ship sweep not on
That should sweep at its swiftest,
Though the wind desired
Behind thee driveth!
May the horse never run
That should run at his most might
When from thy foe's face
Thou hast most need to flee!

May the sword never bite
That thou drawest from scabbard
But and if round thine head
In wrath it singeth!

Then should meet price be paid
For Helgi's slaying
When a wolf thou wert
Out in the wild-wood,
Empty of good things
Empty of gladness,
With no meat for thy mouth
But dead men's corpses!

DAG:
With mad words thou ravest,
Thy wits are gone from thee,
When thou for thy brother
Such ill fate biddest;
Odin alone
Let all this bale loose,
Casting the strife-runes
'Twixt friends and kindred.

Rings of red gold
Will thy brother give thee,
And the stead of Vandil
And the lands of Vigdale;
Have half of the land
For thy sorrow's healing,
O ring-arrayed sweetling
For thee and thy sons!

SIGRUN:
No more sit I happy
At Sevafell;
At day-dawn, at night
Naught love I my life
Till broad o'er the people
My lord's light breaketh;
Till his war-horse runneth
Beneath him hither,
Well wont to the gold bit --
Till my king I welcome.

In such wise did Helgi
Deal fear around
To all his foes
And all their friends
As when the goat runneth
Before the wolf's rage
Filled with mad fear
Down from the fell.

As high above all lords
Did Helgi beat him
As the ash-tree's glory

From the thorn ariseth,
Or as the fawn
With the dew-fell sprinkled
Is far above
All other wild things,
As his horns go gleaming
'Gainst the very heavens.

A barrow was raised above Helgi, but when he came in Valhall, then Odin bade him be lord of all things there, even as he; so Helgi sang --

HELGI:
Now shalt thou, Hunding
For the help of each man
Get ready the foot-bath,
And kindle the fire;
The hounds shalt thou bind
And give heed to the horses,
Give wash to the swine
Ere to sleep thou goest.

A bondmaid of Sigrun went in the evening-tide by Helgi's mound, and there saw how Helgi rode toward it with a great company; then she sang --

BONDMAID:
It is vain things' beguilling
That methinks I behold,
Or the ending of all things,
As ye ride, O ye dead men,
Smiting with spurs
Your horses' sides?

Or may dead warriors
Wend their ways homeward?

THE DEAD:
No vain things' beguiling
Is that thou beholdest,
Nor the ruin of all things;
Though thou lookest upon us,
Though we smite with spurs
Our horses' sides;
Rather dead warriors
May wend their ways homeward.

Then went the bondmaid home, and told Sigrun, and sang --

BONDMAID:
Go out, Sigrun
From Sevafell,
If thou listest to look on
The lord of thy people!
For the mound is uncovered
Thither is Helgi come,
And his wounds are bleeding,
But the king thee biddeth
To come and stay
That stream of sorrow.

So Sigrun went into the mound to Helgi, and sang --

SIGRUN:
Now am I as fain
Of this fair meeting,
As are the hungry

Hawks of Odin,
When they wot of the slaying
Of the yet warm quarry,
Or bright with dew
See the day a-dawning.

Ah, I will kiss
My king laid lifeless,
Ere thou castest by
Thy blood-stained byrny.
O Helgi, thy hair
Is thick with death's rime,
With the dew of the dead
Is my love all dripping;
Dead-cold are the hands
Of the son of Hogni;
How for thee, O my king,
May I win healing?

HELGI:
Thou alone, Sigrun
Of Sevafell,
Hast so done that Helgi
With grief's dew drippeth;
O clad in gold
Cruel tears thou weepest,
Bright May of the Southlands,
Or ever thou sleepest;
Each tear in blood falleth
On the breast of thy lord,
Cold wet and bitter-sharp
Swollen with sorrow.

Ah, we shall drink
Dear draughts and lovely,
Though, we have lost
Both life and lands;
Neither shall any
Sing song of sorrow,
Though in my breast
Be wounds wide to behold:
For now are brides
In the mound abiding;
Kings' daughters sit
By us departed.

Bow Sigrun arrayed a bed in the mound, and sang --

SIGRUN:
Here, Helgi, for thee
A bed have I dight,
Kind without woe,
O kin of the Ylfings!
To thy bosom, O king,
Will I come and sleep soft,
As I was wont
When my lord was living.

HELGI:
Now will I call
Naught not to be hoped for
Early or late
At Sevafell,
When thou in the arms
Of a dead man art laid,
White maiden of Hogni,

Here in the mound:
And thou yet quick,
O King's daughter!

Now needs must I ride
On the reddening ways;
My pale horse must tread
The highway aloft;
West must I go
To Windhelm's bridge
Ere the war-winning crowd
Hall-crower (4) waketh.

So Helgi rode his ways: and the others gat them gone home to the
house. But the next night Sigrun bade the bondwoman have heed of
the mound. So at nightfall, thenas Sigrun came to the mound, she
sang:

SIGRUN:
Here now would he come,
If to come he were minded;
Sigmund's offspring
From the halls of Odin.
O me the hope waneth
Of Helgi's coming;
For high on the ash-boughs
Are the ernes abiding,
And all folk drift
Toward the Thing of the dreamland.

BONDMAID:
Be not foolish of heart,
And fare all alone

To the house of the dead,
O Hero's daughter!
For more strong and dreadful
In the night season
Are all dead warriors
Than in the daylight.

But a little while lived Sigrun, because of her sorrow and trouble. But in old time folk trowed that men should be born again, though their troth be now deemed but an old wife's dotting. And so, as folk say, Helgi and Sigrun were born again, and at that tide was he called Helgi the Scathe of Hadding, and she Kara the daughter of Halfdan; and she was a Valkyrie, even as is said in the Lay of Kara.

ENDNOTES:

(1) Only that part of the song is given which completes the episodes of Helgi Hunding's-bane; the earlier part of the song differs little from the Saga.
(2) Hogni, the father of Dar and Sigrun, had been slain by Helgi in battle, and Helgi had given peace to, and taken oaths of Dag. (3) One of the rivers of the under-world.
(4) Hall-crower, "Salgofnir": lit. Hall-gaper, the cock of Valhall.

PART OF THE LAY OF SIGRDRIFA (1)

Now this is my first counsel,
That thou with thy kin
Be guiltless, guileless ever,
Nor hasty of wrath,
Despite of wrong done --
Unto the dead good that doeth.

Lo the second counsel,
That oath thou swearest never,
But trusty oath and true:
Grim tormenting
Gripes troth-breakers;
Cursed wretch is the wolf of vows.

This is my third rede,
That thou at the Thing
Deal not with the fools of folk;
For unwise man
From mouth lets fall
Worser word than well he wotteth.

Yet hard it is
That holding of peace
When men shall deem thee dastard,
Or deem the lie said soothly;

But woeful is home-witness,
Unless right good thou gettest it.
  Ah, on another day
  Drive the life from out him,
And pay the liar back for his lying.

  Now behold the fourth rede:
  If ill witch thee bideth,
Woe-begatting by the way,
  Good going further
  Rather than guesting,
Though thick night be on thee.

  Far-seeing eyes
  Need all sons of men
Who wend in wrath to war;
  For baleful women
  Bide oft by the highway,
Swords and hearts to soften.

  And now the fifth rede:
  As fair as thou seest
Brides on the bench abiding,
  Let not love's silver
  Rule over thy sleeping;
Draw no woman to kind kissing!

  For the sixth thing, I rede
  When men sit a-drinking
Amid ale-words and ill-words,
  Dead thou naught
  With the drunken fight-staves
For wine stealeth wit from many.

Brawling and drink
  Have brought unto men
Sorrow sore oft enow;
  Yea, bane unto some,
  And to some weary bale;
Many are the griefs of mankind.

For the seventh, I rede thee,
  If strife thou raisest
With a man right high of heart,
  Better fight a-field
  Than burn in the fire
Within thine hall fair to behold.

The eighth rede that I give thee:
  Unto all ill look thou,
And hold thine heart from all beguiling;
  Draw to thee no maiden,
  No man's wife bewray thou,
Urge them not unto unmeet pleasure.

This is the ninth counsel:
  That thou have heed of dead folk
Whereso thou findest them a-field;
  Be they sick-dead,
  Be they sea-dead,
Or come to ending by war-weapons.

Let bath be made
  For such men fordone,
Wash thou hands and feet thereof,
  Comb their hair and dry them

Ere the coffin has them;
Then bid them sleep full sweetly.

This for the tenth counsel:
That thou give trust never
Unto oaths of foeman's kin,
Be'st thou bane of his brother,
Or hast thou felled his father;
Wolf in young son waxes,
Though he with gold be gladdened.

For wrong and hatred
Shall rest them never,
Nay, nor sore sorrow.
Both wit and weapons
Well must the king have
Who is fain to be the foremost.

The last rede and eleventh:
Until all ill look thou.
And watch thy friends' ways ever
Scarce durst I look
For long life for thee, king:
Strong trouble ariseth now already.

ENDNOTES:

(1) This continues the first part of the lay given in Chapter XX
of the Saga; and is, in fact, the original verse of Chapter
XXI.

Sigurd of yore,
Sought the dwelling of Giuki,
As he fared, the young Volsung,
After fight won;
Troth he took
From the two brethren;
Oath swore they betwixt them,
Those bold ones of deed.

A may they gave to him
And wealth manifold,
Gudrun the young,
Giuki's daughter:
They drank and gave doom
Many days together,
Sigurd the young,
And the sons of Giuki.

Until they wended
For Brynhild's wooing,
Sigurd a-riding
Amidst their rout;
The wise young Volsung
Who knew of all ways --
Ah! He had wed her,
Had fate so willed it.

Southlander Sigurd
A naked sword,
Bright, well grinded,

Laid betwixt them;
No kiss he won
From the fair woman,
Nor in arms of his
Did the Hun King hold her,
Since he gat the young maid
For the son of Giuki.

No lack in her life
She wotted of now,
And at her death-day
No dreadful thing
For a shame indeed
Or a shame in seeming;
But about and betwixt
Went baleful fate.

Alone, abroad,
She sat of an evening,
Of full many things
She fall a-talking:
"O for my Sigurd!
I shall have death,
Or my fair, my lovely,
Laid in mine arms.

"For the word once spoken,
I sorrow sorely --
His queen is Gudrun,
I am wed to Gunnar;
The dread Norns wrought for us
A long while of woe."

Oft with heart deep
In dreadful thoughts,
O'er ice-fields and ice-hills
She fared a-night time,
When he and Gudrun
Were gone to their fair bed,
And Sigurd wrapped
The bed-gear round her.

"Ah! Now the Hun King
His queen in arms holdeth,
While love I go lacking,
And all things longed for
With no delight
But in dreadful thought."

These dreadful things
Thrust her toward murder:
-- "Listen, Gunnar,
For thou shalt lose
My wide lands,
Yea, me myself!
Never love I my life,
With thee for my lord --

"I will fare back thither
From whence I came,
To my nighest kin
And those that know me
There shall I sit
Sleeping my life away,
Unless thou slayest
Sigurd the Hun King,

Making thy might more
E'en than his might was!

"Yea, let the son fare
After the father,
And no young wolf
A long while nourish!
For on earth man lieth
Vengeance lighter,
And peace shall be surer
If the son live not."

Adrad was Gunnar,
Heavy-hearted was he,
And in doubtful mood
Day-long he sat.
For naught he wotted,
Nor might see clearly
What was the seemliest
Of deeds to set hand to;
What of all deeds
Was best to be done:
For he minded the vows
Sworn to the Volsung,
And the sore wrong
To be wrought against Sigurd.

Wavered his mind
A weary while,
No wont it was
Of those days worn by,
That queens should flee
From the realms of their kings.

"Brynhild to me
Is better than all,
The child of Budli
Is the best of women.
Yea, and my life
Will I lay down,
Ere I am twinned
From that woman's treasure."

He bade call Hogni
To the place where he bided;
With all the trust that might be,
Trowed he in him.

"Wilt thou bewray Sigurd
For his wealth's sake?
Good it is to rule
O'er the Rhine's metal;
And well content
Great wealth to wield,
Biding in peace
And blissful days."

One thing alone Hogni
Had for an answer:
"Such doings for us
Are naught seemly to do;
To rend with sword
Oaths once sworn,
Oaths once sworn,
And troth once plighted.

"Nor know we on mould,
Men of happier days,
The while we four
Rule over the folk;
While the bold in battle,
The Hun King, bides living.

"And no nobler kin
Shall be known afield,
If our five sons
We long may foster;
Yea, a goodly stem
Shall surely wax.
-- But I clearly see
In what wise it standeth,
Brynhild's sore urging
O'ermuch on thee beareth.

"Guttorm shall we
Get for the slaying,
Our younger brother
Bare of wisdom;
For he was out of
All the oaths sworn,
All the oaths sworn,
And the plighted troth."

Easy to rouse him
Who of naught recketh!
-- Deep stood the sword
In the heart of Sigurd.

There, in the hall,

Gat the high-hearted vengeance;
For he can his sword
At the reckless slayer:
Out at Guttorm
Flew Gram the mighty,
The gleaming steel
From Sigurd's hand.

Down fell the slayer
Smitten asunder;
The heavy head
And the hands fell one way,
But the feet and such like
Aback where they stood.

Gudrun was sleeping
Soft in the bed,
Empty of sorrow
By the side of Sigurd:
When she awoke
With all pleasure gone,
Swimming in blood
Of Frey's beloved.

So sore her hands
She smote together,
That the great-hearted
Gat raised in bed;
-- "O Gudrun, weep not
So woefully,
Sweet lovely bride,
For thy brethren live for thee!

"A young child have I
For heritor;
Too young to win forth
From the house of his foes. --
Black deeds and ill
Have they been a-doing,
Evil rede
Have they wrought at last.

"Late, late, rideth with them
Unto the Thing,
Such sister's son,
Though seven thou bear, --
-- But well I wot
Which way all goeth;
Alone wrought Brynhild
This bale against us.

"That maiden loved me
Far before all men,
Yet wrong to Gunnar
I never wrought;
Brotherhood I heeded
And all bounden oaths,
That none should deem me
His queen's darling."

Weary sighed Gudrun,
As the king gat ending,
And so sore her hands
She smote together,
That the cups arow
Rang out therewith,

And the geese cried on high
That were in the homefield.

Then laughed Brynhild
Budli's daughter,
Once, once only,
From out her heart;
When to her bed
Was borne the sound
Of the sore greeting
Of Giuki's daughter.

Then, quoth Gunnar,
The king, the hawk-bearer,
"Whereas, thou laughest,
O hateful woman,
Glad on thy bed,
No good it betokeneth:
Why lackest thou else
Thy lovely hue?
Feeder of foul deeds,
Fey do I deem thee,

"Well worthy art thou
Before all women,
That thine eyes should see
Atli slain of us;
That thy brother's wounds
Thou shouldest see a-bleeding,
That his bloody hurts
Thine hands should bind."

"No man blameth thee, Gunnar,

Thou hast fulfilled death's measure
But naught Atli feareth
All thine ill will;
Life shall he lay down
Later than ye,
And still bear more might
Aloft than thy might.

"I shall tell thee, Gunnar,
Though well the tale thou knowest,
In what early days
Ye dealt abroad your wrong:
Young was I then,
Worn with no woe,
Good wealth I had
In the house of my brother!

"No mind had I
That a man should have me,
Or ever ye Giukings,
Rode into our garth;
There ye sat on your steeds
Three kings of the people --
-- Ah! That that faring
Had never befallen!

"Then spake Atli
To me apart,
And said that no wealth
He would give unto me,
Neither gold nor lands
If I would not be wedded;
Nay, and no part

Of the wealth apportioned,
Which in my first days
He gave me duly;
Which in my first days
He counted down.

"Wavered the mind
Within me then,
If to fight I should fall
And the felling of folk,
Bold in Byrny
Because of my brother;
A deed of fame
Had that been to all folk,
But to many a man
Sorrow of mind.

"So I let all sink
Into peace at the last:
More grew I minded
For the mighty treasure,
The red-shining rings
Of Sigmund's son;
For no man's wealth else
Would I take unto me.

"For myself had I given
To that great king
Who sat amid gold
On the back of Grani;
Nought were his eyes
Like to your eyen,
Nor in any wise

Went his visage with yours;
Though ye might deem you
Due kings of men.

"One I loved,
One, and none other,
The gold-decked may
Had no doubtful mind;
Thereof shall Atli
Wot full surely,
When he getteth to know
I am gone to the dead.

"Far be it from me,
Feeble and wavering,
Ever to love
Another's love --
-- Yes shall my woe
Be well avenged."

Up rose Gunnar,
The great men's leader,
And cast his arms
About the queen's neck;
And all went nigh
One after other,
With their whole hearts
Her heart to turn.

But then all these
From her neck she thrust,
Of her long journey
No man should let her.

Then called he Hogni
To have talk with him;
"Let all folk go
Forth into the hall,
Thine with mine --
-- O need sore and mighty! --
To wot if we yet
My wife's parting may stay.
Till with time's wearing
Some hindrance wax."

One answer Hogni
Had for all;
"Nay, let hard need
Have rule thereover,
And no man let her
Of her long journey!
Never born again,
May she come back thence!

"Luckless she came
To the lap of her mother,
Born into the world
For utter woe,
TO many a man
For heart-whole mourning."

Upraised he turned
From the talk and the trouble,
To where the gem-field
Dealt out goodly treasure;
As she looked and beheld

All the wealth that she had,
And the hungry bondmaids,
And maids of the hall.

With no good in her heart
She donned her gold byrny,
Ere she thrust the sword point
Through the midst of her body:
On the boister's far side
Sank she adown,
And, smitten with sword,
Still bethought her of redes.

"Let all come forth
Who are fain the red gold,
Or things less worthy
To win from my hands;
To each one I give
A necklace gilt over,
Wrought hangings and bed=gear,
And bright woven weed."

All they kept silence,
And thought what to speak,
Then all at once
Answer gave:
"Full enow are death-doomed,
Fain are we to live yet,
Maids of the hall
All meet work winning."

"From her wise heart at last
The linen-clad damsel,

The one of few years
Gave forth the word:
"I will that none driven
By hand or by word,
For our sake should lose
Well-loved life.

"Thou on the bones of you
Surely shall burn,
Less dear treasure
At your departing
Nor with Menia's Meal (1)
Shall ye come to see me."

"Sit thee down, Gunnar,
A word must I say to thee
Of the life's ruin
Of thy lightsome bride --
-- Nor shall thy ship
Swim soft and sweetly
For all that I
Lay life adown.

"Sooner than ye might deem
Shall ye make peace with Gudrun,
For the wise woman
Shall full in the young wife
The hard memory
Of her dead husband.

"There is a may born
Reared by her mother,
Whiter and brighter

Than is the bright day;
She shall be Swanhild,
She shall be Sunbeam.

"Thou shalt give Gudrun
Unto a great one,
Noble, well-praised
Of the world's folk;
Not with her goodwill,
Or love shalt thou give her;
Yet will Atli
Come to win her,
My very brother,
Born of Budli.

-- "Ah! Many a memory
Of how ye dealt with me,
How sorely, how evilly
Ye ever beguiled me,
How all pleasure left me
The while my life lasted! --

"Fain wilt thou be
Oddrun to win,
But thy good liking
Shall Atli let;
But in secret wise
Shall ye win together,
And she shall love thee
As I had loved thee,
If in such wise
Fare had willed it.

"But with all ill
Shall Atli sting thee,
Into the strait worm-close
Shall he cast thee.

"But no long space
Shall slip away
Ere Atli too
All life shall lose,
Yea, all his weal
With the life of his sons,
For a dreadful bed
Dights Gudrun for him,
From a heart sore laden,
With the sword's sharp edge.

"More seemly for Gudrun,
Your very sister,
In death to wend after
Her love first wed;
Had but good rede
To her been given,
Or if her heart
Had been like to my heart.

-- "Faint my speech groweth --
But for our sake
Ne'er shall she lose
Her life beloved;
The sea shall have her,
High billows bear her
Forth unto Jonakr's
Fair land of his fathers.

"There shall she bear sons,
Stays of a heritage,
Stays of a heritage,
Jonakr's sons;
And Swanhild shall she
Send from the land,
That may born of her,
The may born of Sigurd.

"Her shall bite
The rede of Bikki,
Whereas for no good
Wins Jormunrek life;
And so is clean perished
All the kin of Sigurd,
Yea, and more greeting,
And more for Gudrun.

"And now one prayer
Yet pray I of thee --
That last word of mine
Here in the world --
So broad on the field
Be the burg of the dead
That fair space may be left
For us all to lie down,
All those that died
At Sigurd's death!

"Hang round that burg
Fair hangings and shields,
Web by Gauls woven,

And folk of the Gauls:
There burn the Hun King
Lying beside me.

"But on the other side
Burn by the Hun King
Those who served me
Strewn with treasure;
Two at the head,
And two at the feet,
Two hounds therewith,
And two hawks moreover:
Then is all dealt
With even dealing.

"Lay there amidst us
The right-dight metal,
The sharp-edged steel,
That so lay erst;
When we both together
Into one bed went,
And were called by the name
Of man and wife.

"Never, then, belike
Shall clash behind him
Valhall's bright door
With rings bedight:
And if my fellowship
Followeth after,
In no wretched wise
Then shall we wend.

"For him shall follow
My five bondmaids,
My eight bondsmen,
No borel folk:
Yea, and my fosterer,
And my father's dower
That Budli of old days
Gave to his dear child.

"Much have I spoken,
More would I speak,
If the sword would give me
Space for speech;
But my words are waning,
My wounds are swelling --
Naught but truth have I told --
-- And now make I ending."

ENDNOTES:

(1) "Menia's Maid" -- periphrasis for gold.

THE HELL-RIDE OF BRYNHILD.

After the death of Brynhild were made two bales, one for Sigurd, and that was first burned; but Brynhild was burned on the other, and she was in a chariot hung about with goodly hangings. And so folk say that Brynhild drave in her chariot down along the way to Hell, and passed by an abode where dwelt a certain giantess, and the gia

THE GIANT-WOMAN
"Nay, with my goodwill
Never goest thou
Through this stone-pillared
Stead of mine!
More seemly for thee
To sit sewing the cloth,
Than to go look on
The love of another.

"What dost thou, going
From the land of the Gauls,
O restless head,
To this mine house?
Golden girl, hast thou not,
If thou listest to hearken,
In sweet wise from thy hands
The blood of men washen?"

BRYNHILD
"Nay, blame me naught,
Bride of the rock-hall,
Though I roved a warring
In the days that were;
The higher of us twain
Shall I ever be holden
When of our kind
Men make account."

THE GIANT-WOMAN
"Thou, O Brynhild,
Budli's daughter,
Wert the worst ever born
Into the world;
For Giuki's children
Death hast thou gotten,
And turned to destruction
Their goodly dwelling."

BRYNHILD
"I shall tell thee
True tale from my chariot,
O thou who naught wottest,
If thou listest to wot;
How for me they have gotten
Those heirs of Giuki,
A loveless life,
A life of lies.

"Hild under helm,
The Hlymdale people,
E'en those who knew me,

Ever would call me.

"The changeful shapes
Of us eight sisters,
The wise king bade
Under oak-tree to bear;
Of twelve winters was I,
If thou listest to wot,
When I sware to the young lord
Oaths of love.

"Thereafter gat I
Mid the folk of the Goths,
For Helmgunnar the old,
Swift journey to Hell,
And gave to Aud's brother
The young, gain and glory;
Whereof overwrath
Waxed Odin with me.

"So he shut me in shield-wall
In Skata grove,
Red shields and white
Close set around me;
And bade him alone
My slumber to break
Who in no land
Knew how to fear.

"He set round my hall,
Toward the south quarter,
The Bane of all trees
Burning aloft;

And ruled that he only
Thereover should ride
Who should bring me the gold
O'er which Fafnir brooded.

"Then upon Grani rode
The goodly gold-strewer
To where my fosterer
Ruled his fair dwelling.
He who alone there
Was deemed best of all,
The War-lord of the Danes,
Well worthy of men.

"In peace did we sleep
Soft in one bed,
As though he had been
Naught but my brother:
There as we lay
Through eight nights wearing,
No hand in love
On each other we laid.

"Yet thence blamed me, Gudrun,
Giuki's daughter,
That I had slept
In the arms of Sigurd;
And then I wotted
As I fain had not wotted,
That they had bewrayed me
In my betrothals.

"Ah! For unrest

All too long
Are men and women
Made alive!
Yet we twain together
Shall wear through the ages,
Sigurd and I. --
-- Sink adown, O giant-wife!"

FRAGMENTS OF THE LAY OF BRYNHILD

HOGNI SAID:
"What hath wrought Sigurd
Of any wrong-doing
That the life of the famed one
Thou art fain of taking?"

GUNNAR SAID:
"To me has Sigurd
Sworn many oaths,
Sworn many oaths,
And sworn them lying,
And he bewrayed me
When it behoved him
Of all folk to his troth
To be the most trusty."

HOGNI SAID:
"Thee hath Brynhild
Unto all bale,
And all hate whetted,
And a work of sorrow;

For she grudges to Gudrun
All goodly life;
And to thee the bliss
Of her very body."

******

Some the wolf roasted,
Some minced the worm,
Some unto Guttorm
Gave the wolf-meat,
Or ever they might
In their lust for murder
On the high king
Lay deadly hand.

Sigurd lay slain
On the south of the Rhine
High from the fair tree
Croaked forth the raven,
"Ah, yet shall Atli
On you redden edges,
The old oaths shall weigh
On your souls, O warriors."

Without stood Gudrun,
Giuki's daughter,
And the first word she said
Was even this word:
"Where then is Sigurd,
Lord of the Warfolk,
Since my kin
Come riding the foremost?

One word Hogni
Had for an answer:
"Our swords have smitten
Sigurd asunder,
And the grey horse hangs drooping
O'er his lord lying dead."

Then quoth Brynhild,
Budli's daughter;
"Good weal shall ye have
Of weapons and lands,
That Sigurd alone
Would surely have ruled
If he had lived
But a little longer.

"Ah, nothing seemly
For Sigurd to rule
Giuki's house
And the folk of the Goths,
When of him five sons
For the slaying of men,
Eager for battle,
Should have been begotten!"

Then laughed Brynhild --
Loud rang the whole house --
One laugh only
From out her heart:
"Long shall your bliss be
Of lands and people,
Whereas the famed lord

You have felled to the earth!"

Then spake Gudrun,
Giuki's daughter;
"Much thou speakest,
Many things fearful,
All grame be on Gunnar
The bane of Sigurd!
From a heart full of hate
Shall come heavy vengeance."

Forth sped the even
Enow there was drunken,
Full enow was there
Of all soft speech;
And all men got sleep
When to bed they were gotten;
Gunnar only lay waking
Long after all men.

His feet fell he to moving,
Fell to speak to himself
The waster of men,
Still turned in his mind
What on the bough
Those twain would be saying,
The raven and erne,
As they rode their ways homeward.

But Brynhild awoke,
Budli's daughter,
May of the shield-folk,
A little ere morning:

"Thrust ye on, hold ye back,
-- Now all harm is wrought, --
To tell of my sorrow,
Or to let all slip by me?"

All kept silence
After her speaking,
None might know
That woman's mind,
Or why she must weep
To tell of the work
That laughing once
Of men she prayed.

BRYNHILD SPAKE:
"In dreams, O Gunnar,
Grim things fell on me;
Dead-cold the hall was,
And my bed was a-cold,
And thou, lord, wert riding
Reft of all bliss,
Laden with fetters
'Mid the host of thy foemen."

"So now all ye,
O House of the Niblungs,
Shall be brought to naught,
O ye oath-breakers!

"Think'st thou not, Gunnar,
How that betid,
When ye let the blood run
Both in one footstep?

With ill reward
Hast thou rewarded
His heart so fain
To be the foremost!

"As well was seen
When he rode his ways,
That king of all worth,
Unto my wooing;
How the host-destroyer
Held to the vows
Sworn beforetime,
Sworn to the young king.

"For his wounding-wand
All wrought with gold,
The king beloved
Laid between us;
Without were its edges
Wrought with fire,
But with venom-drops
Deep dyed within."

Thus this song telleth of the death of Sigurd, and setteth forth how that they slew
him without doors; but some say that they slew him within doors, sleeping in his
bed. But the Dutch Folk say that they slew him out in the wood: and so sayeth the
ancient song of Gudrun, that Sigurd and the sons of Giuki were riding to the Thing
whenas he was slain. But all with one accord say that they bewrayed him in their
troth with him, and fell on him as he lay unarrayed and unawares.

THE SECOND OR ANCIENT LAY OF GUDRUN.

Thiodrek the King was in Atli's house, and had lost there the more part of his men: so there Thiodrek and Gudrun bewailed their troubles one to the other, and she spake and said: --

　　　A may of all mays
My mother reared me
Bright in bower;
Well loved I my brethren,
Until that Giuki
With gold arrayed me,
With gold arrayed me,
And gave me to Sigurd.

Such was my Sigurd,
Among the sons of Giuki
As is the green leek
O'er the low grass waxen,
Or a hart high-limbed
Over hurrying deer,
Or glede-red gold
Over grey silver.

Till me they begrudged,
Those my brethren,
The fate to have him,
Who was first of all men;
Nor might they sleep,
Nor sit a-dooming,
Ere they let slay
My well-loved Sigurd.

Grani ran to the Thing,
There was clatter to hear,
But never came Sigurd

Himself thereunto;
All the saddle-girt beasts
With blood were besprinkled,
As faint with the way
Neath the slayers they went.

Then greeting I went
With Grani to talk,
And with tear-furrowed cheeks
I bade him tell all;
But drooping laid Grani,
His head in the grass,
For the steed well wotted
Of his master's slaying.

A long while I wandered,
Long my mind wavered,
Ere the kings I might ask
Concerning my king.

Then Gunnar hung head,
But Hogni told
Of the cruel slaying
Of my Sigurd:
"On the water's far side
Lies, smitten to death,
The bane of Guttorm
To the wolves given over.

"Go, look on Sigurd,
On the ways that go southward,
There shalt thou hear
The ernes high screaming,

The ravens a-croaking
As their meat they crave for;
Thou shalt hear the wolves howling
Over thine husband.

"How hast thou, Hogni,
The heart to tell me,
Me of joy made empty,
Of such misery?
Thy wretched heart
May the ravens tear
Wide over the world,
With no men mayst thou wend."

One thing Hogni
Had for answer,
Fallen from his high heart,
Full of all trouble:
"More greeting yet,
O Gudrun, for thee,
If my heart the ravens
Should rend asunder!"

Thence I turned
From the talk and the trouble
To go a leasing (1)
What the wolves had left me;
No sigh I made
No smote hands together,
Nor did I wail
As other women
When I sat over
My Sigurd slain.

Night methought it,
And the moonless dark,
When I sat in sorrow
Over Sigurd;
Better than all things
I deemed it would be
If they would let me
Cast my life by,
Or burn me up
As they burn the birch-wood.

From the fell I wandered
Five days together,
Until the high hall
Of Half lay before me;
Seven seasons there
I sat with Thora,
The daughter of Hacon,
Up in Denmark.

My heart to gladden
With gold she wrought
Southland halls
And swans of the Dane-folk;
There had we painted
The chiefs a-playing;
Fair our hands wrought
Folk of the kings.

Red shields we did,
Doughty knights of the Huns,
Hosts spear-dight, hosts helm-dight,

All a high king's fellows;
And the ships of Sigmund
From the land swift sailing;
Heads gilt over
And prows fair graven.

On the cloth we broidered
That tide of their battling,
Siggeir and Siggar,
South in Fion.

Then heard Grimhild,
The Queen of Gothland,
How I was abiding,
Weighed down with woe;
And she thrust the cloth from her
And called to her sons,
And oft and eagerly
Asked them thereof,
Who for her son
Would their sister atone,
Who for her lord slain
Would lay down weregild.

Fain was Gunnar
Gold to lay down
All wrongs to atone for,
And Hogni in likewise;
Then she asked who was fain
Of faring straightly,
The steed to saddle
To set forth the wain,
The horse to back,

And the hawk to fly,
To shoot forth the arrow
From out the yew-bow.

Valdarr the Dane-king
Came with Jarisleif
Eymod the third went
Then went Jarizskar;
In kingly wise
In they wended,
The host of the Longbeards;
Red cloaks had they,
Byrnies short-cut,
Helms strong hammered,
Girt with glaives,
And hair red-gleaming.

Each would give me
Gifts desired,
Gifts desired,
Speech dear to my heart,
If they might yet,
Despite my sorrow,
Win back my trust,
But in them nought I trusted.

Then brought me Grimhild
A beaker to drink of,
Cold and bitter,
Wrong's memory to quench;
Made great was that drink
With the might of the earth,
With the death-cold sea

And the blood that Son (2) holdeth.

On that horn's face were there
All the kin of letters
Cut aright and reddened,
How should I rede them rightly?

The ling-fish long
Of the land of Hadding,
Wheat-ears unshorn,
And wild things' inwards.

In that mead were mingled
Many ills together,
Blood of all the wood,
And brown-burnt acorns;
The black dew of the hearth, (3)
And god-doomed dead beasts' inwards
And the swine's liver sodden,
For wrongs late done that deadens.

Then waned my memory
When that was within me,
Of my lord 'mid the hall
By the iron laid low.
Three kings came
Before my knees
Ere she herself
Fell to speech with me.

"I will give to thee, Gudrun,
Gold to be glad with,
All the great wealth

Of thy father gone from us,
Rings of red gold
And the great hall of Lodver,
And all fair hangings left
By the king late fallen.

"Maids of the Huns
Woven pictures to make,
And work fair in gold
Till thou deem'st thyself glad.
Alone shalt thou rule
O'er the riches of Budli,
Shalt be made great with gold,
And be given to Atli."

"Never will I
Wend to a husband,
Or wed the brother
Of Queen Brynhild;
Naught it beseems me
With the son of Budli
Kin to bring forth,
Or to live and be merry."

"Nay, the high chiefs
Reward not with hatred,
For take heed that I
Was the first in this tale!
To thy heart shall it be
As if both these had life,
Sigurd and Sigmund,
When thou hast borne sons."

"Naught may I, Grimhild,
Seek after gladness,
Nor deem aught hopeful
Of any high warrior,
Since wolf and raven
Were friends together,
The greedy, the cruel,
O'er great Sigurd's heart-blood."

"Of all men that can be
For the noblest of kin
This king have I found,
And the foremost of all;
Him shalt thou have
Till with eld thou art heavy --
Be thou ever unwed,
If thou wilt naught of him!"

"Nay, nay, bid me not
With thy words long abiding
To take unto me
That balefullest kin;
This king shall bid Gunnar
Be stung to his bane,
And shall cut the heart
From out of Hogni.

"Nor shall I leave life
Ere the keen lord,
The eager in sword-play,
My hand shall make end of."

Grimhild a-weeping

Took up the word then,
When the sore bale she wotted
Awaiting her sons,
And the bane hanging over
Her offspring beloved.

"I will give thee, moreover,
Great lands, many men,
Wineberg and Valberg,
If thou wilt but have them;
Hold them lifelong,
And live happy, O daughter!"

"Then him must I take
From among kingly men,
'Gainst my heart's desire,
From the hands of my kinsfolk;
But no joy I look
To have from that lord:
Scarce may my brother's bane
Be a shield to my sons."

Soon was each warrior
Seen on his horse,
But the Gaulish women
Into wains were gotten;
Then seven days long
O'er a cold land we rode,
And for seven other
Clove we the sea-waves.
But with the third seven
O'er dry land we wended.

There the gate-wardens
Of the burg, high and wide,
Unlooked the barriers
Ere the burg-garth we rode to --

*****
*****

Atli woke me
When meseemed I was
Full evil of heart
For my kin dead slain.

"In such wise did the Norns
Wake me or now." --
Fain was he to know
Of this ill foreshowing --
"That methought, O Gudrun,
Giuki's daughter,
That thou setst in my heart
A sword wrought for guile."

"For fires tokening I deem it
That dreaming of iron,
But for pride and for lust
The wrath of fair women
Against some bale
Belike, I shall burn thee
For thy solace and healing
Though hateful thou art."

"In the fair garth methought
Had saplings fallen

E'en such as I would
Should have waxen ever;
Uprooted were these,
And reddened with blood,
And borne to the bench,
And folk bade me eat of them.

"Methought from my hand then
Went hawks a-flying
Lacking their meat
To the land of all ill;
Methought that their hearts
Mingled with honey,
Swollen with blood
I ate amid sorrow.

"Lo, next two whelps
From my hands I loosened,
Joyless were both,
And both a-howling;
And now their flesh
Became naught but corpses,
Whereof must I eat
But sore against my will."

"O'er the prey of the fishers
Will folk give doom;
From the bright white fish
The heads will they take;
Within a few nights,
Fey as they are,
A little ere day
Of that draught will they eat."

"Ne'er since lay I down,
Ne'er since would I sleep,
Hard of heart, in my bed: --
That deed have I to do. (4)

ENDNOTES:

(1) The original has "a vid lesa". "Leasing" is the word still
     used for gleaning in many country sides in England.
(2) Son was the vessel into which was poured the blood of
     Quasir, the God of Poetry.
(3) This means soot.
(4) The whole of this latter part is fragmentary and obscure;
     there seems wanting to two of the dreams some trivial
     interpretation by Gudrun, like those given by Hogni to
     Kostbera in the Saga, of which nature, of course, the
     interpretation contained in the last stanza but one is, as
     we have rendered it: another rendering, from the different
     reading of the earlier edition of "Edda" (Copenhagen, 1818)
     would make this refer much more directly to the slaying of
     her sons by Gudrun.

THE SONG OF ATLI.

Gudrun, Giuki's daughter, avenger her brethren, as is told far and wide; first
she slew the sons of Atli, and then Atli himself; and she burned the hall thereafter,
and all the household with it: and about these matters is this song made: --

In days long gone
Sent Atli to Gunnar

A crafty one riding,
Knefrud men called him;
To Giuki's garth came he,
To the hall of Gunnar,
To the benches gay-dight,
And the gladsome drinking.

There drank the great folk
'Mid the guileful one's silence,
Drank wine in their fair hall:
The Huns' wrath they feared
When Knefrud cried
In his cold voice,
As he sat on the high seat,
That man of the Southland:

"Atli has sent me
Riding swift on his errands
On the bit-griping steed
Through dark woodways unbeaten,
To bid thee, King Gunnar,
Come to his fair bench
With helm well-adorned,
To the house of King Atli.

"Shield shall ye have there
And spears ashen-shafted,
Helms ruddy with gold,
And hosts of the Huns;
Saddle-gear silver gilt,
Shirts red as blood,
The hedge of the warwife,
And horses bit-griping.

"And he saith he will give you
Gnitaheath widespread,
And whistling spears
And prows well-gilded,
Might wealth
With the stead of Danpi,
And that noble wood
Men name the Murkwood."

Then Gunnar turned head
And spake unto Hogni:
"What rede from thee, high one,
Since such things we hear?
No gold know I
On Gnitaheath,
That we for our parts
Have not portion as great.

"Seven halls we have
Fulfilled of swords,
And hilts of gold
Each sword there has;
My horse is the best,
My blade is the keenest;
Fair my bow o'er the bench is,
Gleams my byrny with gold;
Brightest helm, brightest shield,
From Kiar's dwelling ere brought --
Better all things I have
Than all things of the Huns."

HOGNI SAID:

"What mind has our sister
That a ring she hath sent us
In weed of wolves clad?
Bids she not to be wary?
For a wolf's hair I found
The fair ring wreathed about;
Wolf beset shall the way be
If we wend on this errand."

No sons whetted Gunnar,
Nor none of his kin,
Nor learned men nor wise men,
Nor such as were mighty.
Then spake Gunnar
E'en as a king should speak,
Glorious in mead-hall
From great heart and high:

"Rise up now, Fiornir,
Forth down the benches
Let the gold-cups of great ones
Pass in hands of my good-men!
Well shall we drink wine,
Draughts dear to our hearts,
Though the last of all feasts
In our fair house this be!

"For the wolves shall rule
O'er the wealth of the Niblungs,
With the pine-woods' wardens
In Gunnar perish:
And the black-felled bears
With fierce teeth shall bite

For the glee of the dog kind,
If again comes not Gunnar."

Then good men never shamed,
Greeting aloud,
Led the great king of men
From the garth of his home;
And cried the fair son
Of Hogni the king:
"Fare happy, O Lords,
Whereso your hearts lead you!"

Then the bold knights
Let their bit-griping steeds
Wend swift o'er the fells,
Tread the murk-wood unknown,
All the Hunwood was shaking
As the hardy ones fared there;
O'er the green meads they urged
Their steeds shy of the goad.

Then Atli's land saw they;
Great towers and strong,
And the bold men of Bikki,
Aloft on the burg:
The Southland folks' hall
Set with benches about,
Dight with bucklers well bounden,
And bright white shining shields.

There drank Atli,
The awful Hun king,
Wine in his fair hall;

Without were the warders,
Gunnar's folk to have heed of,
Lest they had fared thither
With the whistling spear
War to wake 'gainst the king.

But first came their sister
As they came to the hall,
Both her brethren she met,
With beer little gladdened:
"Bewrayed art thou, Gunnar!
What dost thou great king
To deal war to the Huns?
Go thou swift from the hall!

Better, brother, hadst thou
Fared here in thy byrny
Than with helm gaily dight
Looked on Atli's great house:
Them hadst sat then in saddle
Through days bright with the sun
Fight to awaken
And fair fields to redden:

"O'er the folk fate makes pale
Should the Norn's tears have fallen,
The shield mays of the Huns
Should have known of all sorrow;
And King Atli himself
To worm-close should be brought;
But now is the worm-close
Kept but for thee."

Then spake Gunnar
Great 'mid the people:
"Over-late sister
The Niblungs to summon;
A long way to seek
The helping of warriors,
The high lord unshamed,
From the hills of the Rhine!"

*****

*****

Seven Hogni beat down
With his sword sharp-grinded,
And the eighth man he thrust
Amidst of the fire.
Ever so shall famed warrior
Fight with his foemen,
As Hogni fought
For the hand of Gunnar.

But on Gunnar they fell,
And set him in fetters,
And bound hard and fast
That friend of Burgundians;
Then the warrior they asked
If he would buy life,
But life with gold
That king of the Goths.

Nobly spake Gunnar,
Great lord of the Niblungs;
"Hogni's bleeding heart first

Shall lie in mine hand,
Cut from the breast
Of the bold-riding lord,
With bitter-sharp knife
From the son of the king."

With guile the great one
Would they beguile,
On the wailing thrall
Laid they hand unwares,
And cut the heart
From out of Hjalli,
Laid it bleeding on trencher
And bare it to Gunnar.

"Here have I the heart
Of Hjalli the trembler,
Little like the heart
Of Hogni the hardy:
As much as it trembleth
Laid on the trencher
By the half more it trembled
In the breast of him hidden."

Then laughed Hogni
When they cut the heart from him,
From the crest-smith yet quick,
Little thought he to quail.
The hard acorn of thought
From the high king they took,
Laid it bleeding on trencher
And bare it Gunnar.

"Here have I the heart
Of Hogni the hardy,
Little like to the heart
Of Hjalli the trembler.
Howso little it quaketh
Laid here on the dish,
Yet far less it quaked
In the breast of him laid.

"So far mayst thou bide
From men's eyen, O Atli,
As from that treasure
Thou shalt abide!

"Behold in my heart
Is hidden for ever
That hoard of the Niblungs,
Now Hogni is dead.
Doubt threw me two ways
While the twain of us lived,
But all that is gone
Now I live on alone.

"The great Rhine shall rule
O'er the hate-raising treasure,
That gold of the Niblungs,
The seed of the gods:
In the weltering water
Shall that wealth lie a-gleaming,
Or it shine on the hands
Of the children of Huns!"

Then cried Atli,

King of the Hun-folk,
"Drive forth your wains now
The slave is fast bounden."
And straightly thence
The bit-shaking steeds
Drew the hoard-warden,
The war-god to his death.

Atli the great king,
Rode upon Glaum,
With shields set round about,
And sharp thorns of battle:
Gudrun, bound by wedlock
To these, victory made gods of,
Held back her tears
As the hall she ran into.

"Let it fare with thee, Atli,
E'en after thine oaths sworn
To Gunnar fell often;
Yea, oaths sworn of old time,
By the sun sloping southward,
By the high burg of Sigry,
By the fair bed of rest,
By the red ring of Ull!"

Now a host of men
Cast the high king alive
Into a close
Crept o'er within
With most foul worms,
Fulfilled of all venom,
Ready grave to dig

In his doughty heart.

Wrathful-hearted he smote
The harp with his hand,
Gunnar laid there alone;
And loud rang the strings. --
In such wise ever
Should hardy ring-scatterer
Keep gold from all folk
In the garth of his foeman.

Then Atli would wend
About his wide land,
On his steed brazen shod,
Back from the murder.
Din there was in the garth,
All thronged with the horses;
High the weapon-song rose
From men come from the heath.

Out then went Gudrun,
'Gainst Atli returning,
With a cup gilded over,
To greet the land's ruler;
"Come, then, and take it,
King glad in thine hall,
From Gudrun's hands,
For the hell-farers groan not!"

Clashed the beakers of Atli,
Wine-laden on bench,
As in hall there a-gathered,
The Huns fell a-talking,

And the long-bearded eager ones
Entered therein,
From a murk den new-come,
From the murder of Gunnar.

Then hastened the sweet-faced
Delight of the shield-folk,
Bright in the fair hall,
Wine to bear to them:
The dreadful woman
Gave dainties withal
To the lords pale with fate,
Laid strange word upon Atli:

"The hearts of thy sons
Hast thou eaten, sword-dealer,
All bloody with death
And drenched with honey:
In most heavy mood
Brood o'er venison of men!
Drink rich draughts therewith,
Down the high benches send it!

"Never callest thou now
From henceforth to thy knee
Fair Erp or fair Eiril,
Bright-faced with the drink;
Never seest thou them now
Amidmost the seat,
Scattering the gold,
Or shafting of spears;
Manes trimming duly,
Or driving steeds forth!"

Din arose from the benches,
Dread song of men was there,
Noise 'mid the fair hangings,
As all Hun's children wept;
All saving Gudrun,
Who never gat greeting,
For her brethren bear-hardy
For her sweet sons and bright,
The young ones, the simple
Once gotten with Atli.

*****

*****

The seed of gold
Sowed the swan-bright woman,
Rings of red gold
She gave to the house-carls;
Fate let she wax,
Let the bright gold flow forth,
In naught spared that woman
The store-houses' wealth.

Atli unaware
Was a-weary with drink;
No weapon had he,
No heeding of Gudrun --
Ah, the pity would be better,
When in soft wise they twain
Would full often embrace
Before the great lords!

To the bed with sword-point
Blood gave she to drink
With a hand fain of death,
And she let the dogs loose:
Then in from the hall-door --
-- Up waked the house-carls --
Hot brands she cast,
Gat revenge for her brethren.

To the flame gave she all
Who therein might be found;
Fell adown the old timbers,
Reeked all treasure-houses;
There the shield-mays were burnt,
Their lives' span brought to naught;
In the fierce fire sank down
All the stead of the Budlungs.

Wide told of is this --
Ne'er sithence in the world,
Thus fared bride clad in byrny
For her brothers' avenging;
For behold, this fair woman
To three kings of the people,
Hath brought very death
Or ever she died!

THE WHETTING OF GUDRUN.

Gudrun went down unto the sea whenas she had slain Atli, and she cast herself therein, for she was fain to end her life: but nowise might she drown. She drave

over the firths to the land of King Jonakr, and he wedded her, and their sons were
Sorli, and Erp, and Hamdir, and there was Swanhild, Sigurd's daughter, nourished:
and she was given to Jormunrek the Mighty. Now Bikki was a man of his, and gave
such counsel to Randver, the king's son, as that he should take her; and with that
counsel were the young folk well content.

Then Bikki told the king, and the king let hang Randver, but bade Swanhild
be trodden under horses' feet. But when Gudrun heard thereof, she spake to her
sons --

> Words of strife heard I,
> Huger than any,
> Woeful words spoken,
> Sprung from all sorrow,
> When Gudrun fierce-hearted
> With the grimmest of words
> Whetter her sons
> Unto the slaying.

> "Why are ye sitting here?
> Why sleep ye life away?
> Why doth it grieve you nought?
> Glad words to speak,
> Now when your sister --
> Young of years was she --
> Has Jormunrek trodden
> With the treading of horses? --

> "Black horses and white
> In the highway of warriors;
> Grey horses that know
> The roads of the Goths. --

> "Little like are ye grown

To that Gunnar of old days!
Nought are your hearts
As the heart of Hogni!
Well would ye seek
Vengeance to win
If your mood were in aught
As the mood of my brethren,
Or the hardy hearts
Of the Kings of the Huns!"

Then spake Hamdir,
The high-hearted --
"Little didst thou
Praise Hogni's doings,
When Sigurd woke
From out of sleep,
And the blue-white bed-gear
Upon thy bed
Grew red with man's blood --
With the blood of thy mate!

"Too baleful vengeance
Wroughtest thou for thy brethren
Most sore and evil
When thy sons thou slewedst,
Else all we together
On Jormunrek
Had wrought sore vengeance
For that our sister.

"Come, bring forth quickly
The Hun kings' bright gear,
Since thou has urged us

Unto the sword-Thing!"

Laughing went Gudrun
To the bower of good gear,
Kings' crested helms
From chests she drew,
And wide-wrought byrnies
Bore to her sons:
Then on their horses
Load laid the heroes.

Then spake Hamdir,
The high-hearted --
"Never cometh again
His mother to see
The spear-god laid low
In the land of the Goths.
That one arvel mayst thou
For all of us drink,
For sister Swanhild,
And us thy sons."

Greeted Gudrun
Giuki's daughter;
Sorrowing she went
In the forecourt to sit,
That she might tell,
With cheeks tear-furrowed,
Her weary wail
In many a wise.

"Three fires I knew,
Three hearths I knew,

To three husbands' houses
Have I been carried;
And better than all
Had been Sigurd alone,
He whom my brethren
Brought to his bane.

"Such sore grief as that
Methought never should be,
Yet more indeed
Was left for my torment
Then, when the great ones
Gave me to Atli.

"My fair bright boys
I bade unto speech,
Nor yet might I win
Weregild for my bale,
Ere I had hewn off
Those Niblungs' heads.

"To the sea-strand I went
With the Norns sorely wroth,
For I would thrust from me
The storm of their torment;
But the high billows
Would not drown, but bore me
Forth, till I stepped a-land
Longer to live.

"Then I went a-bed --
-- Ah, better in the old days,
This was the third time! --

To a king of the people;
Offspring I brought forth,
Props of a fair house,
Props of a fair house,
Jonakr's fair sons.

"But around Swanhild
Bond-maidens sat,
Her, that of all mine
Most to my heart was;
Such was my Swanhild,
In my hall's midmost,
As is the sunbeam
Fair to beheld.

"In gold I arrayed her,
And goodly raiment,
Or ever I gave her
To the folk of the Goths.
That was the hardest
Of my heavy woes,
When the bright hair, --
O the bright hair of Swanhild! --
In the mire was trodden
By the treading of horses.

"This was the sorest,
When my love, my Sigurd,
Reft of glory
In his bed gat ending:
But this the grimmest
When glittering worms
Tore their way

Through the heart of Gunnar.

"But this the keenest
When they cut to the quick
Of the hardy heart
Of the unfeared Hogni.
Of much of bale I mind me,
Of many griefs I mind me;
Why should I sit abiding
Yet more bale and more?

"Thy coal-black horse,
O Sigurd, bridle,
The swift on the highway!
O let him speed hither!
Here sitteth no longer
Son or daughter,
More good gifts
To give to Gudrun!

"Mindst thou not, Sigurd,
Of the speech betwixt us,
When on one bed
We both sat together,
O my great king --
That thou wouldst come to me
E'en from the hall of Hell,
I to thee from the fair earth?

"Pile high, O earls
The oaken pile,
Let it be the highest
That ever queen had!

Let the fire burn swift,
My breast with woe laden,
And thaw all my heart,
Hard, heavy with sorrow!"

Now may all earls
Be bettered in mind,
May the grief of all maidens
Ever be minished,
For this tale of sorrow
So told to its ending.

THE LAY OF HAMDIR

Great deeds of bale
In the garth began,
At the sad dawning
The tide of Elves' sorrow
When day is a-waxing
And man's grief awaketh,
And the sorrow of each one
The early day quickeneth.

Not now, not now,
Nor yesterday,
But long ago
Has that day worn by,
That ancientest time,
The first time to tell of,
Then, whenas Gudrun,
Born of Giuki,

Whetter her sons
To Swanhild's avenging.

"Your sister's name
Was naught but Swanhild,
Whom Jormunrek
With horses has trodden! --
White horses and black
On the war-beaten way,
Grey horses that go
On the roads of the Goths.

"All alone am I now
As in holt is the aspen;
As the fir-tree of boughs,
So of kin am I bare;
As bare of things longed for
As the willow of leaves
When the bough-breaking wind
The warm day endeth.

"Few, sad, are ye left
O kings of my folk!
Yet alone living
Last shreds of my kin!

"Ah, naught are ye grown
As that Gunnar of old days;
Naught are your hearts
As the heart of Hogni!
Well would ye seek
Vengeance to win
If your hearts were in aught

As the hearts of my brethren!"

Then spake Hamdir
The high-hearted:
"Nought hadst thou to praise
The doings of Hogni,
When they woke up Sigurd
From out of slumber,
And in bed thou sat'st up
'Mid the banes-men's laughter.

"Then when thy bed=gear,
Blue-white, well woven
By art of craftsmen
All swam with thy king's blood;
The Sigurd died,
O'er his dead corpse thou sattest,
Not heeding aught gladsome,
Since Gunnar so willed it.

"Great grief for Atli
Gatst thou by Erp's murder,
And the end of thine Eitil,
But worse grief for thyself.
Good to use sword
For the slaying of others
In such wise that its edge
Shall not turn on ourselves!"

Then well spake Sorli
From a heart full of wisdom:
"No words will I
Make with my mother,

Though both ye twain
Need words belike --
What askest thou, Gudrun,
To let thee go greeting?

"Weep for thy brethren,
Weep for thy sweet sons,
And thy nighest kinsfolk
Laid by the fight-side!
Yea, and thou Gudrun,
May'st greet for us twain
Sitting fey on our steeds
Doomed in far lands to die."

From the garth forth they went
With hearts full of fury,
Sorli and Hamdir,
The sons of Gudrun,
And they met on the way
The wise in all wiles:
"And thou little Erp,
What helping from thee?"

He of alien womb
Spake out in such wise:
"Good help for my kin,
Such as foot gives to foot,
Or flesh-covered hand
Gives unto hand!"

"What helping for foot
That help that foot giveth,
Or for flesh-covered hand

The helping of hand?"

Then spake Erp
Yet once again
Mock spake the prince
As he sat on his steed:
"Fool's deed to show
The way to a dastard!"
"Bold beyond measure,"
Quoth they, "is the base-born!"

Out from the sheath
Drew they the sheath-steel,
And the glaives' edges played
For the pleasure of hell;
By the third part they minished
The might that they had,
Their young kin they let lie
A-cold on the earth.

Then their fur-cloaks they shook
And bound fast their swords,
In webs goodly woven
Those great ones were clad;
Young they went o'er the fells
Where the dew was new-fallen
Swift, on steeds of the Huns,
Heavy vengeance to wreak.

Forth stretched the ways,
And an ill way they found,
Yea, their sister's son (1)
Hanging slain upon tree --

Wolf-trees by the wind made cold
At the town's westward
Loud with cranes' clatter --
Ill abiding there long!

Din in the king's hall
Of men merry with drink,
And none might hearken
The horses' tramping
Or ever the warders
Their great horn winded.

Then men went forth
To Jormunrek
To tell of the heeding
Of men under helm:
"Give ye good counsel!
Great ones are come hither,
For the wrong of men mighty
Was the may to death trodden."

"Loud Jormunrek laughed,
And laid hand to his beard,
Nor bade bring his byrny,
But with the wine fighting,
Shook his red locks,
On his white shield sat staring,
And in his hand
Swung the gold cup on high.

"Sweet sight for me
Those twain to set eyes on,
Sorli and Hamdir,

Here in my hall!
Then with bowstrings
Would I bind them,
And hang the good Giukings
Aloft on the gallows!"

*****

*****

Then spake Hrothglod
From off the high steps,
Spake the slim-fingered
Unto her son, --
-- For a threat was cast forth
Of what ne'er should fall --
"Shall two men alone
Two hundred Gothfolk
Bind or bear down
In the midst of their burg?"

*****

*****

Strife and din in the hall,
Cups smitten asunder
Men lay low in blood
From the breasts of Goths flowing.

Then spake Hamdir,
The high-hearted:
"Thou cravedst, O king,
From the coming of us,
The sons of one mother,

Amidmost thine hall --
Look on these hands of thine,
Look on these feet of thine,
Cast by us, Jormunrek,
On to the flame!"

Then cried aloud
The high Gods' kinsman (2)
Bold under byrny, --
Roared he as bears roar;
"Stones to the stout ones
That the spears bite not,
Nor the edges of steel,
These sons of Jonakr!"

*****

*****

QUOTH SORLI:
"Bale, brother, wroughtst thou
By that bag's (3) opening,
Oft from that bag
Rede of bale cometh!
Heart hast thou, Hamdir,
If thou hadst heart's wisdom
Great lack in a man
Who lacks wisdom and lore!"

HAMDIR SAID:
"Yes, off were the head
If Erp were alive yet,
Our brother the bold
Whom we slew by the way;

The far-famed through the world --
Ah, the fares drave me on,
And the man war made holy,
There must I slay!"

SORLI SAID:
  "Unmeet we should do
  As the doings of wolves are,
Raising wrong each 'gainst other
  As the dogs of the Norns,
  The greedy ones nourished
In waste steads of the world.

In strong wise have we fought,
On Goths' corpses we stand,
Beat down by our edges,
E'en as ernes on the bough.
Great fame our might winneth,
Die we now, or to-morrow, --
No man lives till eve
Whom the fates doom at morning."
At the hall's gable-end
Fell Sorli to earth,
But Hamdir lay low
At the back of the houses.

Now this is called the Ancient Lay of Hamdir.

ENDNOTES:

(1) Randver, the son of their sister's husband.
(2) Odin, namely. (3) "Bag", his mouth.

THE LAMENT OF ODDRUN.

There was a king hight Heidrik, and his daughter was called Borgny, and the name of her lover was Vilmund. Now she might nowise be made lighter of a child she travailed with, before Oddrun, Atil's sister, came to her, -- she who had been the love of Gunnar, Giuki's son. But of their speech together has this been sung:

I have hear tell
In ancient tales
How a may there came
To Morna-land,
Because no man
On mould abiding
For Heidrik's daughter
Might win healing.

All that heard Oddrun,
Atil's sister,
How that the damsel
Had heavy sickness,
So she led from stall
Her bridled steed,
And on the swart one
Laid the saddle.

She made her horse wend
O'er smooth ways of earth,
Until to a high-built
Hall she came;
Then the saddle she had
From the hungry horse,

And her ways wended
In along the wide hall,
And this word first
Spake forth therewith:

"What is most famed,
Afield in Hunland,
Or what may be
Blithest in Hunland?"

QUOTH THE HANDMAID:
"Here lieth Borgny,
Borne down by trouble,
Thy sweet friend, O Oddrun,
See to her helping!"

ODDRUN SAID:
"Who of the lords
Hath laid this grief on her,
Why is the anguish
Of Borgny so weary?"

THE HANDMAID SAID:
"He is hight Vilmund,
Friend of hawk-bearers,
He wrapped the damsel
In the warm bed-gear
Five winters long
Without her father's wotting."

No more than this
They spake methinks;
Kind sat she down

By the damsel's knee;
Mightily sand Oddrun,
Sharp piercing songs
By Borgny's side:

Till a maid and a boy
Might tread on the world's ways,
Blithe babes and sweet
Of Hogni's bane:
Then the damsel forewearied
The word took up,
The first word of all
That had won from her:

"So may help thee
All helpful things,
Fey and Freyia,
And all the fair Gods,
As thou hast thrust
This torment from me!"

ODDRUN SAID:
"Yet no heart had I
For thy helping,
Since never wert thou
Worthy of helping,
But my word I held to,
That of old was spoken
When the high lords
Dealt out the heritage,
That every soul
I would ever help."

BORGNY SAID:
"Right mad art thou, Oddrun,
And reft of thy wits,
Whereas thou speakest
Hard words to me
Thy fellow ever
Upon the earth
As of brothers twain,
We had been born."

ODDRUN SAID:
"Well I mind me yet,
What thou saidst that evening,
Whenas I bore forth
Fair drink for Gunnar;
Such a thing, saidst thou,
Should fall out never,
For any may
Save for me alone."

Mind had the damsel
Of the weary day
Whenas the high lords
Dealt out the heritage,
And she sat her down,
The sorrowful woman,
To tell of the bale,
And the heavy trouble.

"Nourished was I
In the hall of kings --
Most folk were glad --
'Mid the council of great ones:

In fair life lived I,
And the wealth of my father
For five winters only,
While yet he had life.

"Such were the last words
That ever he spake,
The king forewearied,
Ere his ways he went;
For be bade folk give me
The gold red-gleaming,
And give me in Southlands
To the son of Grimhild.

"But Brynhild he bade
To the helm to betake her,
And said that Death-chooser
She should become;
And that no better
Might ever be born
Into the world,
If fate would not spoil it.

"Brynhild in bower
Sewed at her broidery,
Folk she had
And fair lands about her;
Earth lay a-sleeping,
Slept the heavens aloft
When Fafnir's-bane
The burg first saw.

"Then was war waged

With the Welsh-wrought sword
And the burg all broken
That Brynhild owned;
Nor wore long space,
E'en as well might be,
Ere all those wiles
Full well she knew.

"Hard and dreadful
Was the vengeance she drew down,
So that all we
Have woe enow.
Through all lands of the world
Shall that story fare forth
How she did her to death
For the death of Sigurd.

"But therewithal Gunnar
The gold-scatterer
Did I fall to loving
And should have loved him.
Rings of red gold
Would they give to Atli,
Would give to my brother
Things goodly and great.

"Yea, fifteen steads
Would they give for me,
And the load of Grani
To have as a gift;
But then spake Atli,
That such was his will,
Never gift to take

From the sons of Giuki.

"But we in nowise
Might love withstand,
And mine head must I lay
On my love, the ring-breaker;
And many there were
Among my kin,
Who said that they
Had seen us together.

"Then Atli said
That I surely never
Would fall to crime
Or shameful folly:
But now let no one
For any other,
That shame deny
Where love has dealing.

"For Atli sent
His serving-folk
Wide through the murkwood
Proof to win of me,
And thither they came
Where they ne'er should have come,
Where one bed we twain
Had dight betwixt us.

"To those men had we given
Rings of red gold,
Naught to tell
Thereof to Atli,

But straight they hastened
Home to the house,
And all the tale
To Atli told.

'Whereas from Gudrun
Well they hid it,
Though better by half
Had she have known it.

*****

*****

"Din was there to hear
Of the hoofs gold-shod,
When into the garth
Rode the sons of Giuki.

"There from Hogni
The heart they cut,
But into the worm-close
Cast the other.
There the king, the wise-hearted,
Swept his harp-strings,
For the might king
Had ever mind
That I to his helping
Soon should come.

"But now was I gone
Yet once again
Unto Geirmund,
Good feast to make;

Yet had I hearing,
E'en out from Hlesey,
How of sore trouble
The harp-strings sang.

"So I bade the bondmaids
Be ready swiftly,
For I listed to save
The life of the king,
And we let our ship
Swim over the sound,
Till Atli's dwelling
We saw all clearly.

Then came the wretch (1)
Crawling out,
E'en Atli's mother,
All sorrow upon her!
A grave gat her sting
In the heart of Gunnar,
So that no helping
Was left for my hero.

"O gold-clad woman,
Full oft I wonder
How I my life
Still hold thereafter,
For methought I loved
That light in battle,
The swift with the sword,
As my very self.

"Thou hast sat and hearkened

As I have told thee
Of many an ill-fate,
Mine and theirs --
Each man liveth
E'en as he may live --
Now hath gone forth
The greeting of Oddrun."

ENDNOTES:

(1) Atli's mother took the form of the only adder that was not
    lulled to sleep by Gunnar's harp-playing, and who slew him.

The Codes Of Hammurabi And Moses
W. W. Davies

QTY

The discovery of the Hammurabi Code is one of the greatest achievements of archaeology, and is of paramount interest, not only to the student of the Bible, but also to all those interested in ancient history...

Religion   **ISBN:** *1-59462-338-4*   **Pages:132**

MSRP $12.95

The Theory of Moral Sentiments
Adam Smith

QTY

This work from 1749. contains original theories of conscience amd moral judgment and it is the foundation for systemof morals.

Philosophy   ISBN: *1-59462-777-0*   **Pages:536**

MSRP $19.95

Jessica's First Prayer
Hesba Stretton

QTY

In a screened and secluded corner of one of the many railway-bridges which span the streets of London there could be seen a few years ago, from five o'clock every morning until half past eight, a tidily set-out coffee-stall, consisting of a trestle and board, upon which stood two large tin cans, with a small fire of charcoal burning under each so as to keep the coffee boiling during the early hours of the morning when the work-people were thronging into the city on their way to their daily toil...

Childrens   ISBN: *1-59462-373-2*

Pages:84

MSRP $9.95

My Life and Work
Henry Ford

QTY

Henry Ford revolutionized the world with his implementation of mass production for the Model T automobile. Gain valuable business insight into his life and work with his own auto-biography... "We have only started on our development of our country we have not as yet, with all our talk of wonderful progress, done more than scratch the surface. The progress has been wonderful enough but..."

Pages:300

Biographies/   ISBN: *1-59462-198-5*   *MSRP $21.95*

The Art of Cross-Examination
Francis Wellman

QTY

I presume it is the experience of every author, after his first book is published upon an important subject, to be almost overwhelmed with a wealth of ideas and illustrations which could readily have been included in his book, and which to his own mind, at least, seem to make a second edition inevitable. Such certainly was the case with me; and when the first edition had reached its sixth impression in five months, I rejoiced to learn that it seemed to my publishers that the book had met with a sufficiently favorable reception to justify a second and considerably enlarged edition. ..

Reference   ISBN: *1-59462-647-2*

Pages:412

MSRP $19.95

On the Duty of Civil Disobedience
Henry David Thoreau

QTY

Thoreau wrote his famous essay, On the Duty of Civil Disobedience, as a protest against an unjust but popular war and the immoral but popular institution of slave-owning. He did more than write—he declined to pay his taxes, and was hauled off to gaol in consequence. Who can say how much this refusal of his hastened the end of the war and of slavery ?

Law   ISBN: *1-59462-747-9*

Pages:48

MSRP $7.45

Dream Psychology Psychoanalysis for Beginners
Sigmund Freud

QTY

Sigmund Freud, born Sigismund Schlomo Freud (May 6, 1856 - September 23, 1939), was a Jewish-Austrian neurologist and psychiatrist who co-founded the psychoanalytic school of psychology. Freud is best known for his theories of the unconscious mind, especially involving the mechanism of repression; his redefinition of sexual desire as mobile and directed towards a wide variety of objects; and his therapeutic techniques, especially his understanding of transference in the therapeutic relationship and the presumed value of dreams as sources of insight into unconscious desires.

Psychology   ISBN: *1-59462-905-6*

Pages:196

MSRP $15.45

The Miracle of Right Thought
Orison Swett Marden

QTY

Believe with all of your heart that you will do what you were made to do. When the mind has once formed the habit of holding cheerful, happy, prosperous pictures, it will not be easy to form the opposite habit. It does not matter how improbable or how far away this realization may see, or how dark the prospects may be, if we visualize them as best we can, as vividly as possible, hold tenaciously to them and vigorously struggle to attain them, they will gradually become actualized, realized in the life. But a desire, a longing without endeavor, a yearning abandoned or held indifferently will vanish without realization.

Pages:360

Self Help   ISBN: *1-59462-644-8*

MSRP $25.45

The Rosicrucian Cosmo-Conception Mystic Christianity by *Max Heindel* ISBN: *1-59462-188-8* **$38.95**
The Rosicrucian Cosmo-conception is not dogmatic, neither does it appeal to any other authority than the reason of the student. It is, not controversial, but is, sent forth in the, hope that it may help to clear... New Age/Religion Pages 646

Abandonment To Divine Providence by *Jean-Pierre de Caussade* ISBN: *1-59462-228-0* **$25.95**
"The Rev. Jean Pierre de Caussade was one of the most remarkable spiritual writers of the Society of Jesus in France in the 18th Century. His death took place at Toulouse in 1751. His works have gone through many editions and have been republished... Inspirational/Religion Pages 400

Mental Chemistry by *Charles Haanel* ISBN: *1-59462-192-6* **$23.95**
Mental Chemistry allows the change of material conditions by combining and appropriately utilizing the power of the mind. Much like applied chemistry creates something new and unique out of careful combinations of chemicals the mastery of mental chemistry... New Age Pages 354

The Letters of Robert Browning and Elizabeth Barret Barrett 1845-1846 vol II ISBN: *1-59462-193-4* **$35.95**
by *Robert Browning* and *Elizabeth Barrett* Biographies Pages 596

Gleanings In Genesis (volume I) by *Arthur W. Pink* ISBN: *1-59462-130-6* **$27.45**
Appropriately has Genesis been termed "the seed plot of the Bible" for in it we have, in germ form, almost all of the great doctrines which are afterwards fully developed in the books of Scripture which follow... Religion/Inspirational Pages 420

The Master Key by *L. W. de Laurence* ISBN: *1-59462-001-6* **$30.95**
In no branch of human knowledge has there been a more lively increase of the spirit of research during the past few years than in the study of Psychology, Concentration and Mental Discipline. The requests for authentic lessons in Thought Control, Mental Discipline and... New Age/Business Pages 422

The Lesser Key Of Solomon Goetia by *L. W. de Laurence* ISBN: *1-59462-092-X* **$9.95**
This translation of the first book of the "Lemegton" which is now for the first time made accessible to students of Talismanic Magic was done, after careful collation and edition, from numerous Ancient Manuscripts in Hebrew, Latin, and French... New Age/Occult Pages 92

Rubaiyat Of Omar Khayyam by *Edward Fitzgerald* ISBN: *1-59462-332-5* **$13.95**
Edward Fitzgerald, whom the world has already learned, in spite of his own efforts to remain within the shadow of anonymity, to look upon as one of the rarest poets of the century, was born at Bredfield, in Suffolk, on the 31st of March, 1809. He was the third son of John Purcell... Music Pages 172

Ancient Law by *Henry Maine* ISBN: *1-59462-128-4* **$29.95**
The chief object of the following pages is to indicate some of the earliest ideas of mankind, as they are reflected in Ancient Law, and to point out the relation of those ideas to modern thought. Religion/History Pages 452

Far-Away Stories by *William J. Locke* ISBN: *1-59462-129-2* **$19.95**
"Good wine needs no bush, but a collection of mixed vintages does. And this book is just such a collection. Some of the stories I do not want to remain buried for ever in the museum files of dead magazine-numbers an author's not unpardonable vanity..." Fiction Pages 272

Life of David Crockett by *David Crockett* ISBN: *1-59462-250-7* **$27.45**
"Colonel David Crockett was one of the most remarkable men of the times in which he lived. Born in humble life, but gifted with a strong will, an indomitable courage, and unremitting perseverance... Biographies/New Age Pages 424

Lip-Reading by *Edward Nitchie* ISBN: *1-59462-206-X* **$25.95**
Edward B. Nitchie, founder of the New York School for the Hard of Hearing, now the Nitchie School of Lip-Reading, Inc, wrote "LIP-READING Principles and Practice". The development and perfecting of this meritorious work on lip-reading was an undertaking... How-to Pages 400

A Handbook of Suggestive Therapeutics, Applied Hypnotism, Psychic Science ISBN: *1-59462-214-0* **$24.95**
by *Henry Munro* Health/New Age/Health/Self-help Pages 376

A Doll's House: and Two Other Plays by *Henrik Ibsen* ISBN: *1-59462-112-8* **$19.95**
Henrik Ibsen created this classic when in revolutionary 1848 Rome. Introducing some striking concepts in playwriting for the realist genre, this play has been studied the world over. Fiction/Classics/Plays 308

The Light of Asia by *sir Edwin Arnold* ISBN: *1-59462-204-3* **$13.95**
In this poetic masterpiece, Edwin Arnold describes the life and teachings of Buddha. The man who was to become known as Buddha to the world was born as Prince Gautama of India but he rejected the worldly riches and abandoned the reigns of power when... Religion/History/Biographies Pages 170

The Complete Works of Guy de Maupassant by *Guy de Maupassant* ISBN: *1-59462-157-8* **$16.95**
"For days and days, nights and nights, I had dreamed of that first kiss which was to consecrate our engagement, and I knew not on what spot I should put my lips..." Fiction/Classics Pages 240

The Art of Cross-Examination by *Francis L. Wellman* ISBN: *1-59462-309-0* **$26.95**
Written by a renowned trial lawyer, Wellman imparts his experience and uses case studies to explain how to use psychology to extract desired information through questioning. How-to/Science/Reference Pages 408

Answered or Unanswered? by *Louisa Vaughan* ISBN: *1-59462-248-5* **$10.95**
Miracles of Faith in China Religion Pages 112

The Edinburgh Lectures on Mental Science (1909) by *Thomas* ISBN: *1-59462-008-3* **$11.95**
This book contains the substance of a course of lectures recently given by the writer in the Queen Street Hall, Edinburgh. Its purpose is to indicate the Natural Principles governing the relation between Mental Action and Material Conditions... New Age/Psychology Pages 148

Ayesha by *H. Rider Haggard* ISBN: *1-59462-301-5* **$24.95**
Verily and indeed it is the unexpected that happens! Probably if there was one person upon the earth from whom the Editor of this, and of a certain previous history, did not expect to hear again... Classics Pages 380

Ayala's Angel by *Anthony Trollope* ISBN: *1-59462-352-X* **$29.95**
The two girls were both pretty, but Lucy who was twenty-one who was supposed to be simple and comparatively unattractive, whereas Ayala was credited, as her Bombwhat romantic name might show, with poetic charm and a taste for romance. Ayala when her father died was nineteen... Fiction Pages 484

The American Commonwealth by *James Bryce* ISBN: *1-59462-286-8* **$34.45**
An interpretation of American democratic political theory. It examines political mechanics and society from the perspective of Scotsman James Bryce Politics Pages 572

Stories of the Pilgrims by *Margaret P. Pumphrey* ISBN: *1-59462-116-0* **$17.95**
This book explores pilgrims religious oppression in England as well as their escape to Holland and eventual crossing to America on the Mayflower, and their early days in New England... History Pages 268

QTY

The Fasting Cure *by Sinclair Upton*   ISBN: *1-59462-222-1* **$13.95**
In the Cosmopolitan Magazine for May, 1910, and in the Contemporary Review (London) for April, 1910, I published an article dealing with my experiences in fasting. I have written a great many magazine articles, but never one which attracted so much attention... New Age/Self Help/Health Pages 164

Hebrew Astrology *by Sepharial*   ISBN: *1-59462-308-2* **$13.45**
In these days of advanced thinking it is a matter of common observation that we have left many of the old landmarks behind and that we are now pressing forward to greater heights and to a wider horizon than that which represented the mind-content of our progenitors... Astrology Pages 144

Thought Vibration or The Law of Attraction in the Thought World   ISBN: *1-59462-127-6* **$12.95**
by William Walker Atkinson   *Psychology/Religion Pages 144*

Optimism *by Helen Keller*   ISBN: *1-59462-108-X* **$15.95**
Helen Keller was blind, deaf, and mute since 19 months old, yet famously learned how to overcome these handicaps, communicate with the world, and spread her lectures promoting optimism. An inspiring read for everyone... Biographies/Inspirational Pages 84

Sara Crewe *by Frances Burnett*   ISBN: *1-59462-360-0* **$9.45**
In the first place, Miss Minchin lived in London. Her home was a large, dull, tall one, in a large, dull square, where all the houses were alike, and all the sparrows were alike, and where all the door-knockers made the same heavy sound... Childrens/Classic Pages 88

The Autobiography of Benjamin Franklin *by Benjamin Franklin*   ISBN: *1-59462-135-7* **$24.95**
The Autobiography of Benjamin Franklin has probably been more extensively read than any other American historical work, and no other book of its kind has had such ups and downs of fortune. Franklin lived for many years in England, where he was agent... Biographies/History Pages 332

Name	
Email	
Telephone	
Address	
City, State ZIP	

☐ **Credit Card**   ☐ **Check / Money Order**

Credit Card Number	
Expiration Date	
Signature	

Please Mail to: Book Jungle
PO Box 2226
Champaign, IL 61825
or Fax to: 630-214-0564

ORDERING INFORMATION

web: *www.bookjungle.com*
email: *sales@bookjungle.com*
fax: *630-214-0564*
mail: *Book Jungle PO Box 2226 Champaign, IL 61825*
or PayPal *to sales@bookjungle.com*

Please contact us for bulk discounts

DIRECT-ORDER TERMS

**20% Discount if You Order
Two or More Books**
Free Domestic Shipping!
Accepted: Master Card, Visa,
Discover, American Express